AF360593

HINDU LAW AND JUDICATURE

LECTOR HOUSE PUBLIC DOMAIN WORKS

This book is a result of an effort made by Lector House towards making a contribution to the preservation and repair of original classic literature. The original text is in the public domain in the United States of America, and possibly other countries depending upon their specific copyright laws.

In an attempt to preserve, improve and recreate the original content, certain conventional norms with regard to typographical mistakes, hyphenations, punctuations and/or other related subject matters, have been corrected upon our consideration. However, few such imperfections might not have been rectified as they were inherited and preserved from the original content to maintain the authenticity and construct, relevant to the work. The work might contain a few prior copyright references as well as page references which have been retained, wherever considered relevant to the part of the construct. We believe that this work holds historical, cultural and/or intellectual importance in the literary works community, therefore despite the oddities, we accounted the work for print as a part of our continuing effort towards preservation of literary work and our contribution towards the development of the society as a whole, driven by our beliefs.

We are grateful to our readers for putting their faith in us and accepting our imperfections with regard to preservation of the historical content. We shall strive hard to meet up to the expectations to improve further to provide an enriching reading experience.

Though, we conduct extensive research in ascertaining the status of copyright before redeveloping a version of the content, in rare cases, a classic work might be incorrectly marked as not-in-copyright. In such cases, if you are the copyright holder, then kindly contact us or write to us, and we shall get back to you with an immediate course of action.

HAPPY READING!

HINDU LAW AND JUDICATURE

YÁJNAVALKYA,
EDWARD RÖER,
WILLIAM AUSTIN MONTRIOU

ISBN: 978-93-89821-95-6

Published: 1859

© 2020
LECTOR HOUSE LLP

LECTOR HOUSE LLP
E-MAIL: lectorpublishing@gmail.com

HINDU LAW AND JUDICATURE

FROM THE DHARMA-ŚÁSTRA
OF YÁJNAVALKYA

IN ENGLISH

WITH EXPLANATORY NOTES
AND INTRODUCTION

BY

**EDWARD RÖER, PH. D., M. D.
AND W. A. MONTRIOU, BARRISTER.**

1859.

PREFACE.

The immediate incentive to this undertaking was, a knowledge, or at least a strong impression, that a connected and explanatory translation of the rules of jurisprudence[1] in the Dharma Śástra of Yájnavalkya was a practical want.

Such impression was coincided in, and therefore proved correct, by a long list of local subscribers eminently qualified, by position and experience, to decide.

Dr. Röer is responsible for the fidelity of the rendering, so far as depends on knowledge of the Sanscrit language and literature, of Hindu mythology and philosophy. Mr. Montriou has aided, so far as enabled by juridical acquirements and experience. The language of translation has, therefore, been a joint labour, often the result of much and anxious discussion, and, if not unfrequently but a choice of doubtful alternatives, yet, always a choice made with pains and circumspection.

The text we have generally followed is Stenzler's[2] which is based on and selected from two MSS. in the royal library at Berlin and two editions published in Calcutta.[3]

We have not neglected constant comparison with Stenzler's German translation as well as with the several detached passages as translated by Colebrooke and W. Macnaghten.

Words within brackets ([ ]) are not in the original text.

References to, and extracts from, the standard commentary upon Yájnavalkya, the Mitákshará, necessarily form the staple of our notes. All such extracts are distinguished by the initial (*M.*), and the author of the commentary we invariably refer to as, the Commentator.

At the same time, we have not blindly or implicitly followed this commentator. In some sense all Hindu glosses are untrustworthy guides. They assume the text to be the language of inspiration; and, as the several Dharma Śástras not merely differ, but often dispose of the same subject in a contradictory manner, Pandits deem it their duty to reconcile all discrepancies, how forced soever their interpretations may be. In passages so dealt with, we have endeavoured to give the plain meaning of the original text.

We gratefully acknowledge the obliging assistance, in research, enquiry, and suggestion, occasionally afforded, in the progress of our task, by Babus, Chandra

[1] *vyavahára.*

[2] Yájnavalkya›s Gesetzbuch, Sanscrit and Deutsch, Berlin and London, 1849.

[3] 1. Sanhitá of Yájnavalkya, edited by Sri Bhavánícharana Vandyopádhyaya: 2. The text published in the Mitákshará Dharma Śástra, Calcutta, 1812.

Saikhur Dev[4] and Shyámácharaṇa Sircar.[5]

E. R.
W. A. M.

August 1858.

---

[4] Formerly head superintendent of the legal and zemindarry affairs of the maharajah of Burdwan.

[5] Joint chief translator and interpreter H. M. Supreme Court.

INTRODUCTION.

Professor Stenzler enumerates[6] forty-six distinct Dharma Śástras or recognised codes of Hindu law and ritual, *scil.*

†††	1.	Agni.	††	24.	Prachetas.
.†	2.	Angiras.	†††	25.	Prajápati.
†	3.	Atri.	†††	26.	Budha.
†	4.	Ápastamba.	†	27.	Brihaspati.
†	5.	Uśanas.	††	28.	Baudháyana.
††	6.	Rishyaśringa.	††	29.	Bhrigu.
††	7.	Kaśyapa.	†	30.	Manu.
†	8.	Kátyáyana.	††	31.	Maríchi.
††	9.	Kuthumi.	†	32.	Yama.
††	10.	Gárgya.	†	33.	Yájnavalkya.
†	11.	Gautama.	†	34.	Likhita.
†††	12.	Chyavana.	††	35.	Laugákshi.
†††	13.	Ch'hágaleya.	†	36.	Vaśishṭha.
†††	14.	Játúkarṇa.	††	37.	Viśwámittra.
††	15.	Jábáli.	†	38.	Vishṇu.
†	16.	Daksha.	†	39.	Vyása.
††	17.	Devala.	†	40.	Śankha.
††	18.	Nárada.	†	41.	Śátátapa.
†	19.	Paráśara.	†††	42.	Śáṭyáyana.
††	20.	Páraskara.	†	43.	Samvartta.
†††	21.	Pitámaha.	††	44.	Sumantu.
††	22.	Pulastya.	†††	45.	Soma.
††	23.	Paiṭhínasi.	†	46.	Hárita.

Of the above list, twenty (distinguished by one cross) are in Yájnavalkya's list:[7] seventeen of these are named by Paráśara, *viz.* all except Yama, Brihaspati and Vyása, instead of whom he gives Kaśyapa, Gárgya and Prachetas: the *Padma*

[6] See his paper *Zur Geschichte der Indischen Gesetzbücher* (Contributions to the history of the Indian law-books) in Weber's *Indische Studien*, vol. I, pp. 232 to 246.

[7] Yájnavalkya, ch. I, sl. 3 to 5.

Purána gives those named by Yájnavalkya, with the exception of Atri, and seventeen others, (distinguished by two crosses) three of whom, Prachetas, Kaśyapa and Gárgya, are on Paráśara's list, and the remaining fourteen, not before mentioned: Madhusúdana Saraswatí names the same nineteen of Yájnavalkya's list, also Devala, Nárada, Paithínasi: Ráma Krishna, in his gloss to the *Grihya Sútras* of Práskara, mentions thirty-nine, of whom nine (distinguished by three crosses) are new ones. There is also a Dharma Śástra attributed to Sankha and Likhita jointly, thus making forty-seven in the whole. The professor considers all to be extant; and has himself met with quotations from all, except Agni, Kuthumi, Budha, Śátyáyana, and Soma.

To those may be added several recensions of the same Dharma Śástras, of which professor Stenzler speaks to having read of twenty-two.

The entire forty-seven are independent sources of and authorities upon Hindu law.

The Digest of Jagannát'ha Tarcapanchánana, as translated by Colebrooke, is a valuable repertory of texts; but, detached and isolated as they necessarily are, those texts can with difficulty be appreciated or applied.

Yájnavalkya is second in importance to Manu alone: and, with the commentary, is the leading authority of the Mithilá school.

The resident of British India needs not to be informed, that the orthodox Hindu regards his Dharma Śástras as direct revelations of the Divine will: still less need such an one be told, that, among this people, law is entirely subservient to the mysterious despotism of cast,[8] a religious, rather than a political ordinance.

With the Hindu, all religious tenets and aspirations are centred in the idea of BRAHMA, the one, pervading, illimitable substance, without multiple, division or repetition. This idea has two modes or phases, 1st. as representing the absolute, self-included Brahmá; 2nd. as representing Brahmá in connection with, relative to, the world. In the latter, Brahmá is creator of the world, or, the very world, a semblance or a development of the former, the absolute idea. Man's highest aspiration and aim is, to know Brahmá absolutely: to have attained this knowledge implies a total renunciation of worldly concerns, to coalesce with, to be ultimately absorbed in, reunited with, Brahmá. Bráhmanas are held to possess, to represent, this knowledge. Again, Brahmá is the creator, the preserver, also, the objects created and preserved. Kshattriyas represent Brahmá, the preserver: Vaisyás, Brahmá the preserved. The dogma is otherwise explained: in the secondary or relative notion, Brahmá is *Sattwa, Rajas, Tamas, i. e.* goodness, activity, darkness, — respectively represented by the Bráhmana, Kshattriya, and Vaisyá casts.

When the Hindus dwelt in the country of the five rivers, and were worshippers of the powers and phenomena of material Nature, as of Indra, Váyu, Agni &c., cast was necessarily unknown, for the notion of Brahmá was undeveloped.

The divisions or classes among them were conventional; there were princes,

---

[8] We have followed Mr. Elphinstone (Hist. ch. 1) in the orthography of this word: it is from the Portuguese *casta*, breed, race.

priests, and peasants or cultivators.

But class distinction had not then crystallized into cast, into immiscible, uncongenial yet co-ordinate elements of a so called revealed constitution.

So soon however as the idea of Brahmá had attained fixity in the Hindu mind, and simultaneously with it, cast was developed, as we find it (but imperfectly) in the earliest records of Hindu philosophy, the Upanishads.

Thus, cast governs and is antecedent to law, which must bend and adapt itself to cast, as the overruling, intrinsic, unalterable condition of Hinduism, of Hindu life. There is one law, one phase of obligation for the twice-born, another for the Súdrá. In Manu, cast is not so fully and severely developed: Manu permits to the Bráhmaṇa four wives, of whom one may be a Súdrá, necessarily permitting, therefore, a transition or quasi-amalgamation between the highest and the lowest in the scale. Yájnavalkya permits this Bráhmaṇical communion with the Kshattriya and Vaisyá, but not with the Súdrá. Later promulgators of law,[9] restrict the Bráhmaṇa to his own class.

But although cast, once developed, admitted not of change, juridical rules, subservient to cast, might and did progress: civil laws and procedure became more comprehensive and exact, the criminal code more regulated, lenient, and enlightened. And as universally, (for such is human,) breaches and occasional disregard of rules have, silently though surely, worked a change, or caused exceptional accessions to the rules themselves.

The rule of the Sástras, that kingly power should belong to the Kshattriya alone, was, even in the halcyon days of Hindu polity, repeatedly set aside. Chandragupta, a Súdrá, and his dynasty, held sway over India from 315 to 173 B. C.: afterwards came Bráhmaṇical kings, the Kánwas, from 66 to 21 B. C.: whilst the mighty Gupta kings, from 150 to 280 A. C., were Vaisyás.

The code of Manu presents a disarranged mass of regulations, in so much that some have supposed the disorder to have been designed.

That conclusion, however, is repelled by the comparatively succinct arrangement of Yájnavalkya and other sages. It is more consistent to suppose, that Manu, as originally promulgated, was, from time to time, added to, with an accidental disregard of method.

Áchára, ritual, comprises the distinctive cast-ceremonies, domestic and social usages, rites of purification, of sacrifice.

Vyavahára, may be called the juridical rules, embracing as well substantive law as the procedure and practice of legal tribunals.

Práyaschitta, expiations, are the religious sanctions, or penalties of sin; the divine visitation upon offenders, and the mode in which the sinner may avert, by atonement, the consequences of divine vengeance.

The date of Yájnavalkya's Dharma Sástra is not definitely or satisfactorily fixed. From internal evidence, it is doubtless much subsequent to Manu.

---

[9] See Lassen's *Indische Alterthumskunde,* vol. II, p. 510.

The data for conjecturing the period of Yájnavalkya are;

1. Reference is made to Buddhist habits and doctrines, *viz.* the yellow garments, the baldhead, the Swabháva (B. I. sl. 271, 272, and 349).

Hence, this Dharma Sástra must have been promulgated later than B. C. 500.

2. Reference is made to a previous Yoga Sástra promulgated by Yájnavalkya (B. III, sl. 110). Now, the Yoga philosophy was first shaped into a system by Patanjali who, according to Lassen, probably flourished about 200 B. C.

3. Mention is made of coin as *nánáka* (B. II, sl. 240). Now, the word *nano* occurs on the coins of the Indoscythian king, Kanerki, who, according to Lassen, reigned until 40 A. C.

The result, though indefinite, places the earliest date of Yájnavalkya's code towards the middle of the first century after Christ.

CONTENTS

Page

- PREFACE. v
- INTRODUCTION. vii

SELECTED SLOKAS OF THE FIRST BOOK.

- RITUAL AND MORAL CONDUCT.. 1

THE SECOND BOOK

- LAW AND JUDICATURE. 6

SELECTED SLOKAS OF THE FIRST BOOK.
RITUAL AND MORAL CONDUCT.[10]

1. The Munis[11] after adoration to Yájnavalkya, lord of Yogís,[12] thus addressed him:

Reveal to us the several duties of the casts, of the orders,[13] and of the others![14]

2. The prince of the Yogís, who then abode in Mithilá, meditating for a moment, said to the Munis: Hearken to the rules of duty in the country of the black antelope![15]

3. There are fourteen repositories[16] of the sciences and of law; the four Vedas together with the Puráṇas, the Nyáya, the Mimánsá, the Dharma Śástras, and the six Angas.[17]

---

[10] This is the general subject and title of the first book; but the following slokas are selected as introductory of and with reference to civil and municipal law.

[11] Pre-eminent, divine sages; probably the great Rishis, the first-created of Brahmá, mentioned in the opening verse of Manu.

In the third book (sl. 186—189) two classes of Munis are described, of whom one, after blessed experience of Heaven, return to Earth, and the other are to continue in the abodes of bliss until the destruction of the universe. These latter are the publishers of the Vedas, Upanishads, Sútras, Puráṇas, in fine of all records of knowledge through the medium of language.

[12] These (according to Hindu notions) have withdrawn their senses from external things by, as it were, mental concentration, fixing the thoughts, without change or wavering, upon the soul in its relations with the Supreme Being.

[13] *viz.*—the *brahmachári*, the student of the Vedas,

    the *grihastha*, the head of a family.

    the *vánaprastha*, who has retired from active life, to the forest.

    the *sanyásí*, whose duty it is to pass his time in meditating upon Brahmá, so as to attain to the state of a Yogí.

[14] *i. e.* the mixed casts. (*M.*)

[15] Manu, ch. 2, sl. 23.

[16] The Commentator explains this by a word which signifies cause or source.

[17] IV. *Vedas*, of which there are four, each being divided into *sanhitá* and *bráhmaṇa*.

V. *Puráṇas*, these (of which there are 18) treat of the origin and destruction of the world, mythological stories and genealogies, and the doings of the early Hindu monarchs.

VI. *Nyáya*, one of the six orthodox systems of Hindu philosophy, treating especially of logic and dialectics.

4. Manu, Atri, Vishṇu, Háríta, Yájnavalkya, Uśanas, Angiras, Yama, Ápastamba, Sanvarta, Kátyáyana, Brihaspati,

5. Paráśara, Vyása, Śankha, Likhita, Daksha, Gautama, Śátátapa, and Vaśishṭha,[18] are they who have promulgated Dharma Śástras.

6. When a gift is made, in due season, place and manner, in good faith and to a fit person—all this gives the idea of Law.

7. The Śruti, the Smriti,[19] the practice of good men, what seems good to one's self,[20] and a desire maturely considered—these are declared to be the root[21] of Law.

9. Four learned in the Vedas and in the Law form a Court, or Traividya.[22] Whatever is declared by this [Court], or by a single person who has, in an eminent degree, knowledge of the soul in its relations[23]—the same should be [held as] Law.

10. Bráhmaṇs, Kshattriyas, Vaisyás and Śúdrás are the casts: of them the three first are twice-born; all their rites, commencing with the procreative rites, and ending with those [which are gone through] where the corpse is disposed of,[24] are with Mantras.[25]

VII. *Mimánsá*, there are two Mimánsás: the first (*pūrva*) treats of the rules of duty, as derived from the Vedas, the second or subsequent (*uttara*) treats of Brahmá, the universal cause and soul.

VIII. *Dharma Śástras, viz.* Manu, Yájnavalkya, &c., the subject being divided into, 1. Ritual and moral conduct (*áchára*); 2. Law and judicature (*vyavahára*); 3. Expiations (*práyaschitta*).

XIV. *Angas*, six treatises, *viz.*, pronunciation, grammar, prosody, explanation of obscure terms, religious rites, astronomy. These are considered appendants of the Vedas. The word *angas* signifies, limbs.

[18] To these twenty many others have to be added, Nárada, &c.: see Introduction.

[19] Śruti are the Vedas; Smriti, the Dharma Śástras: such is the definition of Manu, ch. 2, sl. 10.

[20] The Commentator qualifies this indefinite source of law, as applicable only where two or more lawful alternatives are presented.

[21] Further explained by the Commentator, the evidence or proofs of law; and he adds, the several proofs mentioned, where they clash, are of weight and authority according to their precedence, *e.g.* Śruti the highest, the mature desire the lowest, Manu, ch. 2, sl. 6, 12.

[22] Which means, having knowledge of the three Vedas. See Manu, ch. 12, sl. 110 to 113.

[23] To explain or enlarge upon this metaphysical phrase would be out of place in the present work. The curious student can refer to the Upanishads and the Vedánta.

[24] Which, in the time of our author, meant, the place of cremation. In the third book, sl. 1, 2, Yájnavalkya says:—A child under two years of age is to be buried, nor shall water be offered; every other deceased, being followed by his relatives to the place for disposal of the dead, shall there be burned.

It was certainly otherwise at the period of the Vedas (vide *Die Todtenbestattung im indischen Alterthum. German Oriental Society's Journal, Vol. VIII. pp.* 467—475): the paraphrase in the text is the meaning of the term used, *smasána.*

[25] Texts of the Vedas to be recited on solemn occasions. See analogous passage, Manu ch. 2, sl. 16.

14. In the eighth year from conception, or in the eighth [of birth],[26] the investiture[27] of the Bráhman [takes place]; of Rajas[28] in the eleventh; of Vaisyás in the twelfth: some [have said, this varies] in accordance with [the usage of] the family.

39. Bráhmans, Kshattriyas, and Vaisyás are born, first, of their mothers, and, a second time, by the girding on of the sacred thread—therefore are they declared to be twice-born.

116. [Men] are to be honoured in the gradation following,—in respect of learning, conduct, years, family, property. Even a Śúdrá, if he excel in these respects, is in old age worthy of honour.

326. The monarch, at his rising [from the night's repose], having seen to the [general] safety, shall himself inspect the [account of] revenue and disbursements; he shall then adjudicate law-suits; after which, having bathed,[29] he may, at his pleasure, take his meal.[30]

342. Of a newly subjugated territory, the monarch shall preserve the social and religious usages, also the judicial system and the state of classes as they already obtain.[31]

352. A ruler, a minister, people, a stronghold, treasure, [power of] punishment, and allies—because these are its elements, a realm is called seven-limbed.

353. When possessed of this, let a monarch cause punishment to fall on the guilty; for, of old, justice was created by Brahmá under the form of punishment.[32]

357. A brother even, or a son, any one to whom respect is due, a father-in-law or maternal uncle, if he transgress, is not to go unpunished by the monarch.

358. The monarch who punishes such as deserve punishment, who slays such as deserve death: he is as one who has made many sacrifices with valuable offerings.[33]

359. Every day should the monarch, pondering on his reward (such as sacrifices gain), himself investigate law-suits in their order with the judges around him.

360. The monarch, always duly correcting [those among] the casts, the mixed classes, the guilds, the schools[34] [of the learned], and the people [in general], who have deviated from their duty, should set them in the [right] path.

---

[26] So we supply the hiatus in the text, in conformity with the opinion of the Commentator. Manu makes no allusion to the alternative, ch. 2, sl. 36.

[27] Induction into the character and privileges of his cast, by means of the sacred thread.

[28] who, being Kshattriyas, here represent the cast.

[29] at mid-day. (*M.*)

[30] Manu ch. 7, sl. 216.

[31] ibid, 201 et seq.

[32] ibid, 13, 41.

[33] Manu ch. 8, sl. 306.

[34] The Commentator explains the general expression here used by the word *haituka*, of which one meaning is that given in the text, but it also signifies, those who do not believe in the Vedas.

361. A particle of dust in the sunbeams, as they shine through a window, is held to consist of three atoms; eight of those [particles] are equal to a poppy seed, of which three are equal to a black mustard seed;

362. Three of these to a white mustard seed, three of these to a barley seed of middle size, three of these to a Krishṇala berry,[35] five of these to a Másha,[36] sixteen of these to a Suvarṇa.[37]

363. A Pala is four or five[38] Suvarṇas. Two Krishṇalas are a silver Másha; sixteen of the latter, a Dharaṇa.

364. A Śatamána and a Pala are each equal to ten Dharaṇas: a Nishka is four Suvarṇas: a copper Paṇa is of the weight of a Karsha.[39]

365. One thousand and eighty Paṇas is declared the highest fine; half of that amount the medium fine; and half of this the lowest fine.

---

[35] *retti* or *gunja*, a shrub bearing a small red and black berry. Wilson.

[36] A sort of kidney bean, *phasealus radiatus*. Wilson.

[37] About 176 grains Troy weight. Wilson.

[38] Manu says four.

[39] These tables of weight, as further explained by the Commentator, may be given thus:

3	Atoms	= 1	Mote.
8	Motes	= 1	Poppy seed or a nit.
3	Poppy seeds or 3 nits	= 1	Black mustard seed.
3	Black mustard seeds	= 1	White mustard seed.
3	White mustard seeds	= 1	Barley corn.
3	Barley corns	= 1	Krishṇala.

Gold.

5	Krishṇalas	= 1	Másha.
16	Máshas	= 1	Suvarṇa.
4	Suvarṇas	= 1	Pala.

Silver.

2	Krishṇalas	= 1	Másha.
16	Máshas	= 1	Dharaṇa.
10	Dharaṇas	= 1	Pala or Śatamána.
4	Suvarṇas	= 1	Nishka.

Copper.

4	Karshas	= 1	Pala.
1	Paṇa	= 1	Karsha *i. e.* 1/4 Pala.

They by no means satisfactorily define the intrinsic weight and signification of the Paṇa, which, as the measure of pecuniary penalty, would seem to be the chief if not sole object of their introduction.

In the corresponding slokas of Manu, ten Palas are said to be equivalent to one Dharaṇa. We can only reconcile this by supposing Manu to refer to a gold Pala and Yájnavalkya to a silver Pala.

366. Reproof, words of ignominy, fine, and death,[40] shall be administered, singly or together, according to the crime.[41]

367. [The monarch] having informed himself of the crime, the place where, and the time when [committed], the strength [of the criminal, his] age, calling, and means, shall cause punishment to fall upon the guilty.[42]

∵ The foregoing extracts, it will have been observed, are of general application, and do not refer to any part of the law in detail. Several slokas in the first book, however, and some in the third, do refer to and affect the details of law, which are the proper subject of the second book, where therefore they are inserted, according to their subject.

---

[40] The Commentator remarks, that this includes every kind of corporal punishment.

[41] Manu, ch. 8, sl. 129, 130.

[42] ibid, sl. 126, also ch. 7, sl. 16. In the last passage, Sir Wm. Jones has added to the term, strength, *his own*; this we consider to be an error, at any rate it is not a mere translation, and we have applied the term used, *viz. strength* simpliciter, differently.

THE SECOND BOOK
LAW AND JUDICATURE.

1. Let the monarch,[43] free from anger or thought of gain, in conjunction with learned bráhmaṇs, adjudicate law-suits, according to the Dharma Śástras.

2. He shall appoint judges perfect in the Vedas and in science,[44] versed in the Dharma Śástras, such as speak truth and bear themselves alike to friend and foe.

3. If the monarch, from press of other business, cannot adjudicate, he shall appoint a bráhmaṇ versed in the whole law, [to preside] with the judges.[45]

4. Should the judges, from partiality, from love of gain, or from fear, act in any-wise contrary to law or usage;[46] each one [so acting] shall be amerced in double the value of the suit.

5. When one who is aggrieved by others, in any way contrary to law or usage, makes a representation to the monarch; this is matter for a law-suit.

6. The representation, as made by the plaintiff, is to be put in writing, in presence of the defendant; the year, month, half-month, day, names, cast, &c.,[47] being given.

7. The answer [of the defendant] to what he has heard [read] is then to be put in writing, in presence of him who made the first representation: and then the latter shall, at once, furnish a statement in writing of the proof to support what he has asserted.

8. This being established, he succeeds in his suit; otherwise, the reverse. Thus it appears, the procedure in law-suits has four steps.

9. Let not a counter-complaint be preferred until the [original] complaint is disposed of, nor let a third person [sue] him against whom a complaint is pend-

---

[43] Various terms are used by our author to denote the head of the State (*e.g.* Rájá, Protector of men, Lord of men, &c.) to suit the metre or fancifully. In translation we have thought it better to be uniform.

[44] What is understood by science is explained in the first book sl. 3.

[45] Manu, ch. 8, sl. 9.

[46] The original is, *smriti ádi* (the second word being equivalent to &c.), which the Commentator explains, as translated, law and usage, or custom.

[47] The &c. signifies, description of chattels, with their number, also particulars of place and time. (*M.*)

ing.[48] The statement of the cause of suit is not to be varied.[49]

10. [The defendant] may bring a counter-plaint for abusive language,[50] or personal trespass,[51] or for acts of atrocious violence.[52] On behalf of each party, a surety, competent to meet the result of the suit, shall be bound.

11. One against whom, after [a plea of] denial, judgment is given, shall pay the amount [adjudged to the plaintiff] together with an equal sum to the monarch.[53] One who has made a false complaint, shall forfeit double the amount of his claim.

12. In a case of atrocious violence, of theft, of reviling or personal trespass,[54] where a cow is the subject, or a [malicious] charge of crime,[55] or an offence destructive of life or property[56] where a female [of the household] is the subject—[in each of these cases] the Court shall compel the parties to go to trial forthwith. In other cases, a day may be appointed at pleasure.

13. One who moves from place to place,[57] who licks the corners of his mouth, whose forehead sweats, and whose countenance changes colour.

14. who with words from a dry throat, stammering, says much that is contradictory, who makes no response to word or look, who contracts the lips—

15. whosoever [in this wise] changes his natural manner, in the action of his

---

[48] The Commentator has enabled us to supply the ellipsis, but he does not fully explain the author's meaning. It would seem, that in those primitive times, it was considered harsh or inexpedient to harass a defendant, or accused person with two legal proceedings, of any sort, at the same time. The sentence will, however, bear the sense, that no stranger or intervener shall be permitted to come in and interrupt the progress of a pending suit.

[49] The Commentator, observing that this prohibition would seem to be implied in the terms of the sixth sloka, explains (on the authority of Nárada) that the latter refers only to the general object of the suit, *e.g.*, that if his verbal complaint be of a loan of money, his recorded complaint shall not be of a loan of apparel—but that this clause, in the ninth sloka, ensures further uniformity in the description of the grievance and character of the suit, *e.g.*, where one has originally complained of retention of 100 pieces of money lent, he shall not vary his complaint to a forcible taking of 100 pieces.

[50] These are expressed by one word, *kalaha*: but the Commentator notes its comprehensive character, as we have translated it. See the analogous passage in Manu, ch. 8, sl. 6, where an equally ambiguous word *párushya* is similarly explained in the text itself. The term rendered "slander" by Sir Wm. Jones is simply, reviling or verbal abuse.

[51] These are expressed by one word, *kalaha*: but the Commentator notes its comprehensive character, as we have translated it. See the analogous passage in Manu, ch. 8, sl. 6, where an equally ambiguous word *párushya* is similarly explained in the text itself. The term rendered "slander" by Sir Wm. Jones is simply, reviling or verbal abuse.

[52] *sáhasa*, explained by the Commentator, assault by means of poison, or any instrument destructive of life. The word has another and more particular signification, as infra sl. 230.

[53] Manu (ch. 8, sl. 59) inflicts a fine of double the debt upon the mendacious debtor.

[54] *párushya*, explained by the Commentator *kalaha*: see note[*].

[55] We have followed the Commentator in rendering these terms, which are very general and indefinite.

[56] We have followed the Commentator in rendering these terms, which are very general and indefinite.

[57] *i. e.* restlessly before the Court.

mind, of his speech, and of his person, is to be set down as false in his complaint, or [if a witness] in his testimony.[58]

16. One who enforces by his own arbitrary act a claim which is denied, who absconds, or who does not respond when called — [each of these] is considered to have failed, and is amenable to punishment.[59]

17. Where there are [rival claims, and] witnesses on both sides, the witnesses of him who asserts the elder title, are to be [first] examined: if that title be admitted,[60] then the witnesses of him who claims by subsequent title [shall be examined].[61]

18. Should the suit be accompanied by a wager, [the Court] shall compel the losing party to pay the fine [prescribed],[62] as well as his wager and his debt to the creditor.

19. Let the monarch, rejecting subtleties, conduct the trial of suits upon the merits: even merits, in the absence of proof, must fail of success in the suit.

20. If one plead a denial to a representation including several matters,[63] and one part be proved against him, the monarch shall compel him to pay the whole amount claimed: but what has not been previously declared [by the plaintiff][64] is

[58] Manu ch. 8, sl. 25, 26.

[59] ibid, sl. 55, 56.

[60] Literally "put down," *i. e.* taken for granted, all question of it disposed of. See next note.

[61] This sloka is by no means unambiguous: but it is satisfactorily explained by the Commentator, who says: "What course is to be adopted where two parties simultaneously present themselves to the Court and tender proofs? *e.g.* A man acquired a field by gift, and, having for some time possessed it, departed with his family to another country: then, another person obtained a gift of the same field, and, having possessed it awhile, was likewise obliged to go to another country. Both parties return at the same time, claim the same field, and resort to a Court of law. Then arises the question, — whose proofs shall be taken? Yájnavalkya says (ut supra sl. 17); that is to say, where one sets up an older title, saying — I was possessed of this field at such a date — his witnesses are the first to be examined; but should the other party urge — True, the field was acquired and enjoyed by him at the first, but the king bought it of him and granted it to me — or — Another got the field and gave it to me; in that case, as the proofs of him who has the older title are of no consequence, and thus he is disposed of, the witnesses of the other claimant are to be examined. It is incorrect [to read the sloka as asserting] that, where there is a denial [of a claim] the witnesses of the plaintiff shall be examined, and where a former judgment or something as a ground of defence is set up, in [either of] which cases the original claim is met, then the witnesses of the defendant shall be heard; inasmuch as all this is included in the rule, — (here the Commentator quotes the 7th sloka of the text). This view is clearly supported by Nárada, *viz.* On a denial, proof is upon the plaintiff; where some ground of defence is stated, upon the defendant; upon an allegation of prior decree, the decree shall be the proof. — After this Nárada proceeds: — When there are two claimants, if there be witnesses, the witnesses of the prior claimant shall be [first examined] — So we perceive, this [description of] law-suit is distinguished from all others." These quotations favor the supposition, that the science of special-pleading is not of European origin, and is traceable to a remote antiquity.

[62] Supra sl. 11.

[63] *e.g.* that the defendant has got possession of gold and silver and apparel, &c. (*M.*)

[64] Supra, sl. 6. The Commentator excludes from the operation of the harsh rule in this 20th sloka, an heir, who is supposed to deny his ancestor's debt or liability through igno-

inadmissible.

21. If two texts of the Law be opposed to each other, an argument founded on usage is of force; but the Dharma Śástra is of greater force than the Artha Śástra.[65] This is a settled rule.

22. Legal proofs are described as, writing, possession, and witnesses.

In the absence of either of those, it is ordained, that some one of the ordeals is [to be resorted to.]

23. In all disputes where property is concerned, the last act is of greater force;[66] except in [cases of] pledge, gift,[67] and sale, when the first act is of greater force.[68]

24. If one see[69] his land in the possession of another[70] and say nothing, it is lost after twenty years; moveables after ten years:[71]

25. excepting pledges, boundary-limits, deposits with specification,[72] prop-

rance; but he attempts to justify the rule itself by experience of human conduct.

[65] This Śástra teaches a system or science of ethics such as moralists now-a-days designate as Machiavellian or jesuitical; in which right or wrong have a relative but little intrinsic meaning.

The Artha Śástra is to be found in the writings of Uśanas, of Brihaspati and others.

[66] A special-pleading signification is given to this dogma by the Commentator: *viz.*

"In questions of debt, &c., though the prior act have been proved, yet a second act may be more important; *e.g.* if one prove that another by borrowing has incurred debt, and the other prove that the money borrowed has been repaid." (*M.*)

[67] The word in the original is, acceptance: but this is evidently used as the concluding act of the transaction referred to, *scil.* gift.

[68] *e.g.* if one, for a consideration, pledge a field to another, and then pledge the same field to some one else, also for a consideration—the first act is the valid one. (*M.*)

[69] Sir Wm. Jones and other learned persons would seem to have restricted the term here used (*pashyati*) to personal knowledge by sight; but it comprehends every mode of personal and actual observation or discovery.

[70] who has no legal connection with it. (*M.*)

[71] The Commentator quotes Nárada, *scil.* "The guilty one who holds possession without title, for even many hundred years, should be punished by the monarch as a thief"— and he endeavours to reconcile with this the law of Yájnavalkya, by confining the latter to the fruits or profits of the land withheld. But this construction cannot be admitted. There is a curious document germane to the subject of this sloka copied in the official notes of Sir Robert Chambers (Chief Justice of the Calcutta Supreme Court) in July 1791. It is a letter from Sir William Jones to the Governor of Bombay upon the Hindu title by adverse possession or prescription. Sir William writes, that the doctrine of the Mitákshará is; "An absolute property may be acquired in land by continued and undisputed possession for twenty years, in the presence of the owner, provided that the possessor came in by a fair title, either by descent or purchase; if he had no fair title, the intermediate profits only are irrecoverable, but the property is not lost." And he concludes; "I only add for your further satisfaction, that, if three descents have happened since the first possession, without a fair title, property is lost, even though the owner was absent; but if three descents have not been cast, an adverse possession for a hundred years gives an absolute property in the land to the possessor, unless the owner was under some legal disability." These may have been the modifications of a later age: they are not to be found in Manu or in Yájnavalkya. Manu ch. 8, sl. 147, &c.

[72] any thing delivered for safe-keeping, its quality and quantity being made known.

erty of idiots and children, deposits without specification,[73] property of the monarch, of women, and of those learned in the Vedas.

26. One who appropriates[74] a pledge, &c., shall be compelled to restore to the owner his property, and to pay a fine of equal value, or according to his means,[75] to the monarch.

27. Acquisition by title[76] is stronger[77] than possession, unless this has come down from ancestors;[78] but acquisition by title is of no avail without possession for a short time.[79]

28. If one holding by title have it questioned [in a Court of justice], he must establish it by proof: but not so his son, nor his son's son; in their case, possession is of greater weight.

29. If one whose title is questioned die [pending the suit[80]], his heir must establish it by proof; in such case possession without title will not avail.[81]

30. Those appointed by the monarch,[82] communities,[83] guilds,[84] and families, have authority, one after the other,[85] to investigate law-suits among men.

31. The monarch shall annul decisions of suits which have been brought about by force or fraud; also those made by women, those made at night, those made in private chambers, those made in a place beyond the limits,[86] and those made by enemies.

(*M.*)

[73] explained infra, sloka 65.

[74] The word literally or usually means "takes away"; and the Commentator explains—where a pledgee retains and refuses to give back the pledge, relying upon his long possession. The &c. refers to the other exceptions in sloka 25.

[75] The Commentator considers the force and intent of this qualification to be, to make the fine commensurate with the usurper's means, with a view rather of enhancing it to the wealthy than of moderating it to the poor, who are perhaps less likely to offend in this wise.

[76] gift, sale, &c. (*M.*)

[77] as proof of ownership, (*M.*) Manu, ch. 8, sl. 200.

[78] for three generations. (*M.*)

[79] Possession is proof when attended with five incidents; a title, length of time, continuance, absence of counter-claim, knowledge of the adverse party. (*M.*)

[80] This qualification is the Commentator's.

[81] Between this and the succeeding sloka another is introduced in the text of the Calcutta edition; *viz.* Possession accompanied by a clear title is proof; possession unaccompanied by a clear title is no proof.—We have omitted this, because the Commentator quotes it as a saying of Nárada, and because it is not found (as vouched by professor Stenzler) in either of the M.S.S. in the Berlin Royal Library.

[82] *scil.* as directed in sloka 2.

[83] By a community (*puga*) is meant, the body of inhabitants of any village or place, without reference to cast or occupation. (*M.*)

[84] A guild (*sreni*) signifies those of one calling, whether of the same cast or not. (*M.*)

[85] Literally "before, before," which implies their successive rank and importance, *i. e.* that an appeal lies from the family to the guild, and so on.

[86] Literally "outside." The Commentator explains it—outside of the town, &c.

32. A suit instituted by one intoxicated, or insane, or stricken with disease,[87] or given up to vice,[88] or a minor, or one under the influence of fear, &c.,[89] or one having no interest, is invalid.

33. When lost property is found,[90] it shall be restored by the monarch to the owner: if the claimant fail to identify by some sign, he shall pay an equivalent fine.

34. If the monarch find a treasure,[91] he shall give half of it to the twice-born.[92] If, on the other hand, a twice-born [find a treasure], he shall, if learned, take the whole, for he is lord of all.[93]

35. Of treasure found by any one else,[94] the monarch shall take a sixth.[95] If the finder do not make report, but [his discovery] comes to light, he shall surrender [what he has found], and shall, besides, be punished.

36. Stolen property, however, is to be given up by the monarch to the subject; seeing that, if he do not give it, he shall bear all the sin of that person from whom [it is stolen].[96]

37. Where there is a pledge, the interest, month by month, shall be an eightieth part; otherwise, two, three, four or five parts, in a hundred, according to the order of cast.[97]

38. They however who travel in forests[98] give ten parts; they who go to sea, twenty parts, in a hundred. Or, all[99] must render to all, of whatever cast, the rate of interest settled amongst themselves.[100]

---

[87] *ártta* out of health; evidently meaning here, the victim of disease so as to be unfit for the business of life.

[88] The word (*vyasani*) may also be rendered, suffering calamity; and the Commentator explains the use made of it in the text to be, a person who is unhappy either by reason of the absence of the object of his desire or by reason of the presence of what is disagreeable to him. We have however preferred the alternative meaning which the word admits of.

[89] &c., *i. e.* paralysed by any cause or emotion whatever. See Manu, ch. 8, sl. 163.

[90] by public officers and delivered to the king. (*M.*)

[91] The Commentator considers the treasure-trove here alluded to, to be buried wealth, of which there is no claimant.

[92] Manu, ch. 8, sl. 37, 38.

[93] The Commentator explains—of the whole world!

[94] *i. e.* by any other than the monarch or a *learned* bráhmaṇ. (*M.*)

[95] The Commentator (referring to Vaśishṭha and Gautama) reads this,—the finder shall take a sixth, the monarch the residue—such being the converse of the plain language used.

[96] Manu ch. 8, sl. 40: in which, to the monarch who fails to make restitution is imputed the guilt of the thief. Sir Wm. Jones' translation of this passage is too indefinite.

[97] *i. e.* The bráhmaṇ borrower gives two hundredths, the kshattriya three hundredths, &c. (*M.*) But Jagannát'ha, in his Digest (Colebrooke, B. 1, c. 1, s. 28) interprets the text inversely, *viz.* the bráhmaṇ creditor takes two *suvarṇas* in a hundred, the kshattriya three, and so on. Manu, ch. 8, sl. 140-142.

[98] where there is risk of life or property. (*M.*)

[99] as well bráhmaṇs as others, (*M.*) Manu ch. 8, sl. 157.

[100] *scil.* Notwithstanding the above provisions of the law, where nothing is expressly stipulated, whatever interest is contracted for must be given and taken.

39. But for cattle and women lent [the return] is, their offspring: the highest encrease demandable for use of liquids[101] is eight-fold; for wearing apparel, for corn, and for gold, four-fold, three-fold and two-fold respectively.

40. The monarch should not blame one who enforces a recognised debt.[102] If he, against whom the debt is enforced, complain to the monarch, he may be punished, besides being compelled to pay the debt.

41. The debtor [as a general rule] shall be made to pay his creditors in the order in which he has received from them; but a bráhman he is to pay [first], and, after him, the monarch.

42. The debtor shall be made to pay to the monarch ten parts in a hundred of the sum proved against him;[103] and the creditor, when he has recovered his property, five parts.[104]

43. One of inferior cast,[105] who is without means, may be compelled to labour[106] in discharge of his debt; but a bráhman,[107] wanting means [to discharge his debt at once], shall pay gradually in proportion to what may come to him.

44. If one do not accept restitution of his property on loan when offered, it is to be delivered to some third party; from which time it ceases to carry interest.

45. A debt incurred by undivided kinsmen on account of the family shall be discharged by the heirs of the head of the family, should the latter die or leave the country.[108]

46. A woman has not to pay a debt incurred by her husband or by her son, nor a father the debt of his son; except such debts be incurred on account of the family: and it is the same with a husband [in respect of a debt] incurred by his wife.

47. A son has not to pay, in this world, his father's debt incurred for spirituous liquor,[109] or, for gratification of lust, or in gambling, nor a fine, nor what remains unpaid of a toll; nor [shall he make good] idle gifts.[110]

48. As to debts of wives of herdsmen, distillers, players, washermen and hunters, the husbands have to pay; because their maintenance depends upon their wives.

49. A debt acknowledged,[111] one incurred by her jointly with her husband,

---

[101] oil, ghee, &c. (*M.*)

[102] Manu enumerates five modes of enforcing or recovering a debt; persuasion, lawsuits, artifice, worrying, force: ch. 8, sl. 49.

[103] as a fine. (*M.*)

[104] to defray the cost of adjudication. (*M.*)

[105] This includes one of equal cast (*M.*) Manu ch. 8, sl. 177; also ch. 9, sl. 229.

[106] in conformity with the usages of his class. (*M.*)

[107] This includes every debtor of superior cast to the creditor. (*M.*)

[108] This rule of course (as observed by the Commentator) includes the head or manager of the family himself, if alive. Manu, ch. 8, sl. 166.

[109] for drinking. (*M.*)

[110] *e.g.* what is promised to a flatterer, a mountebank, a panegyrist, a prize-fighter, &c. (*M.*) Manu ch. 8, sl. 159.

[111] The Commentator explains this to mean, an acknowledgment by the husband on

one incurred by herself [solely][112]—these must be paid by the wife; none other need be paid by her.

50. If a father have gone abroad, or died, or been subdued by calamity,[113] his debt shall be paid by his sons and grandsons;[114] on their denial,[115] the debt must be proved by witnesses.

51. He who takes the property of one who leaves no [capable][116] son, shall pay the debts; so, he who takes[117] the widow; also that son whose paternal estate no other has appropriated, [and who in such case shall always be deemed] fit to inherit property;[118] and if one die without any son, then, whosoever succeeds to the property.

52. To become surety, to be indebted, and to give evidence, is unlawful between brothers, between husband and wife, or between father and son; except, where they are separated in property.

53. Giving surety is enjoined for appearance, for confidence,[119] and for payment.[120] If there be a failure of either of the first two, the surety [himself] in each case shall pay; of the third, his sons [also] must pay.

54. If surety for appearance or for confidence die, the sons have not to pay; of a surety for payment, the sons have to pay.[121]

55. If there are several sureties, they shall pay the debt according to their respective liabilities: if all have undertaken for the entire debt,[122] they shall [severally be made to] pay at the option of the creditor.

56. If a surety be compelled by process of law[123] to discharge the debt, the [principal] debtors shall reimburse him double the amount paid.

---

his death-bed or when about to go abroad.

[112] Colebrooke's translation of this passage adds "or son," but this is unauthorised either by the text or the Commentary.

[113] The Commentator adduces in illustration, his being afflicted with incurable disease.

[114] and this, notwithstanding they are wholly without patrimony or estate derived from their father. (*M.*)

[115] that there is such a debt.

[116] capable of inheriting and managing. (*M.*)

[117] *i. e.* marries.

[118] This is the reading sanctioned by the Commentator, *viz. putro' nanya'sritadravyah*, signifying, that, on failure of those before designated, a son who would be otherwise incapable, by reason of blindness, &c. is to be deemed capable. Another reading may be, as suggested by the Commentator, *putro nú'aya'sritadraoyah*, "not the son whose paternal estate another holds," which is adopted by Colebrooke, and by his author, Jagannát'ha, (Dig. B. 1, ch. 5, s. 171)

[119] *e.g.* "Give such a one money, he will not deceive you; he is the son of such a one." (*M.*)

[120] "If he do not pay, I will." (*M.*)

[121] Manu ch. 8, sl. 160-162.

[122] metaphorically in the original "If all stand under the same shade:" The Commentator explains.

[123] lit. "publicly."

57. For [use of] women and cattle, the offspring shall be given: for corn, [a return of] three fold; for apparel, four fold; for liquids, eight fold.

58. [The owner's property in] a pledge is forfeited if it be not redeemed when the debt is doubled; of one made for a definite period, it is forfeited at the specified date. [The property in] a pledge with usufruct[124] does not become forfeit.

59. If a [simple] pledge be put to use, no interest is [demandable]: so it is if a pledge with usufruct be damaged. If the pledge be wholly spoiled or be destroyed, it must be replaced; except where caused by accident,[125] or by the monarch.[126]

60. A pledge is complete upon acceptance.[127] If the thing pledged have become worthless, although [duly] cared for, either another shall be given [in its place], or the creditor shall receive back his money.

61. If a pledge be [given or taken, in reliance] upon character,[128] the debtor shall be made to pay with interest: the debtor shall be made to repay two-fold, if he received on his plighted word.[129]

62. If one come [and pay his debt], the pledge shall be released; otherwise he [who has the pledge] is a thief:[130] should the creditor be absent, the debtor is to receive back his pledge upon paying the debt to the family;[131]

63. Or it may remain where it was, without interest [on the debt], the value at that date [of the thing pledged] being ascertained. If the debtor fail to come, the creditor may sell [the pledge] before witnesses.

64. If the debt secured by pledge have become doubled, the pledge shall be

[124] as of a field, garden, &c. (*M.*) Manu, ch. 8, sl. 143.

[125] fire, water, &c. (*M.*)

[126] The Commentator excludes from this exception a culpable act of the monarch, but the text is general.

[127] Even though there be a written memorial of the pledge, and attested; yet, without actual acceptance and possession, it is incomplete. (*M.*)

[128] *charitrabandhakam. charitra* (the mode or the subject of pledge) is defined by the Commentator to be either, moral worth, or, the merit earned by performance of religious rites, such as ablution in the Ganges, &c. We have rendered it as the mode, not subject, of pledge. See Jagannát'ha's Digest (Colebrooke), Bk. 1, ch. 3, sec. 2, text cxxiv.

[129] Receiving on one's plighted word (*satyankára*) signifies, borrowing on a solemn promise to repay. The application is, — where, at the time of handing over the pledge, it was expressly declared by the debtor, that the loan should be repaid, even if increased to two-fold the original sum, and the pledge not abandoned; in such case also, the debtor should be made to repay twice the amount of the debt contracted.(*M.*)

The Commentator adds another meaning or application of the latter words of this sloka, in which, reciting the first part, *viz.*, pledging upon the guarantee of character, or, a pledge of religious merit, he goes on to say — It is here laid down, that one who receives on his word, *scil.* words ratifying a bargain of sale and purchase, &c., for instance, receiving a gold ring, &c., as earnest, shall be made to repay twice the value of the thing so given, on breach of the contract: if the party depositing the ring, &c., break off the bargain, he forfeits what he gave as earnest; if the other party break off, he is to be compelled to refund double the value of the earnest received by him.

[130] punishable as a thief. (*M.*)

[131] to one of the family who is a fit person. (*M.*)

released; provided, the [value of the] usufruct of the thing pledged be double [the amount of] the loan.[132]

65. *Upanidhi* is something in a box delivered to the hands of another, without a declaration. This shall be restored in the same manner [as it was given].[133]

66. But one shall not be compelled to make good that of which he has been deprived by the monarch, by accident, or by thieves.[134] When the loss occurs after demand has been made, and the deposit not returned, the depositee is to make it good and to pay a fine of equal value.

67. Whoever of his own accord uses [this description of deposit] shall be fined, and must restore it, together with the profit made.

The same rule applies to things borrowed[135] [for a special occasion], also to what is delivered for the purpose of being restored to the owner,[136] also to what is deposited [in the absence of the head, with the other members of the family],[137] also to the deposits called *nikshepa*,[138] and the like.[139]

68. Those proper to be witnesses are, religious devotees,[140] they who bestow liberally, the wellborn, they who speak truth, they whose chief aim it is to be virtuous,[141] they who are strait in their conduct, they who have sons, and the wealthy.[142]

69. There should be at least three witnesses, such as observe the rites prescribed by the Śruti and the Smriti, and are of a class, whether mixed or unmixed,[143] corresponding [with that of the person who produces them]: otherwise,[144] any person may be a witness for any person.

---

[132] The Commentator implies, that where the usufruct has done more than this, still the transaction is closed by return of the pledge.

[133] Manu, ch. 8, sl. 180.

[134] 90 ibid, sl. 189.

[135] *yáchita, e.g.* ornaments, clothes, &c. lent on occasion of festivals. (*M.*)

[136] *anváhita.* We have followed the Commentator in translating this indefinite term.

[137] This qualification too is the Commentator's. The term used *nyása* is simply, a deposit.

[138] which are those given in the presence of (*i. e.* personally to) the depositee. (*M.*)

[139] such as gold &c. given to be worked (*M.*)

[140] *tapaswí*, the third in rank of the Hindu religious orders.

[141] The four objects of living being, in the creed of the Hindu, virtue, wealth, pleasure, and final liberation of the soul.

[142] Manu, ch. 8, sl. 62, 63.

[143] The terms used are *játi* and *varṇa* which are somewhat ambiguous; but the sense is evidently as rendered, and is so explained by the Commentator. Manu adds,—Women should be witnesses for women, ch. 8, sl. 68.

[144] *i. e.* if the regular and more appropriate witnesses are not available. (*M.*)

After sloka 69 the Calcutta edition has the following:—Those learned in the Vedas, ascetics, the aged, devotees, and the like, are incompetent witnesses, because so declared by law; no other ground [of incompetency] is assigned.

We do not insert this additional sloka for the reasons stated in note[†] supra.

70. Women, minors, aged men,[145] gamblers, persons intoxicated, madmen,[146] persons under suspicion of crime, stageplayers, infidels,[147] forgers, persons who are deprived of any sense,

71. heinous offenders,[148] intimate friends,[149] parties interested [in the suit], confederates, enemies [to either party], thieves, violent characters, the openly wicked,[150] persons cast off [by their friends and kin], and such like,[151] are inadmissible as witnesses.

72. Even one person,[152] being an intelligent follower of ritual duties,[153] may, with the consent of both parties, be witness [sufficient].

All are admissible[154] as witnesses in cases of rape, theft[155] defamation and personal trespass.[156]

73. The judge shall thus address the witnesses, as they come up to the plaintiff and defendant:

The worlds appointed for criminals, for atrocious criminals;[157]

---

[145] of not less than eighty years.(*M.*)

[146] possessed of devils. (*M.*) The expression used by the Commentator may be also translated—under planetary influence.

[147] which the Commentator explains *nirgranthi prabhritayah*, by which probably are indicated those of the Hindu community who disbelieve the Vedas, *e.g.* the Jains.

[148] the slayer of bráhmaṇ, and such heinous criminals. (*M.*) Manu ch. 11, sl. 54. See Note[‡].

[149] of either party. Perhaps this might be rendered, partisans, or, allies.

[150] Said by the Commentator to allude to notorious liars.

[151] *scil.* as found in the other Smritis. The Commentator (quoting Nárada) gives a more detailed account of persons excluded or exempt from giving testimony. Manu ch. 8, sl. 64—67.

[152] a fortiori two persons, (*M.*)

[153] or, who knows the Dharma.

[154] The Commentator excludes from this enabling exception those under moral (not merely arbitrary or conventional) disability, as, criminals. Manu, ch. 8, sl. 72.

[155] also, murder. (*M.*)

[156] *párushya* and *sáhasa*: v. supra in notes[§] et[¶].

[157] Who these are is described by Yájnavalkya, in the third book, *scil.*

sl. 227. The slayer of a bráhmaṇ, the drinker of what intoxicates, the thief, one who violates his *guru's* bed, are great criminals—also, whoever associates with such persons.

sl. 228. Grossly to revile one's *guru*, speaking reproachfully of the Vedas, to slay a friend, after reading from the Veda to forget it,—these [sins] are like to the murder of a bráhmaṇ.

sl. 229. To eat forbidden food, a crooked insincere mode of dealing, a multitude of lying words, kissing the mouth of a menstruous woman,—these [sins] are like to drinking intoxicating liquor.

sl. 230. To steal horses, jewels, men, women, land, cows, property pledged,—these [sins] are like to the stealing of gold.

sl. 231. To debauch a friend's wife, a maiden, a sister, a woman of the lowest grade, a female relative, a son's wife,—these [sins] are recorded as equivalent to violation of a *guru's* bed.

74. the worlds appointed for incendiaries, for murderers of women and children—all these shall be the portion of him who gives false testimony!

75. Know, that whatever good has been done by thee in a hundred former births, all shall become his whom thou defeatest by falsehood![158]

76. That man who withholds his testimony, the monarch shall compel to pay, on the forty-sixth day, the entire debt, as well as a fine equivalent to a tenth of the amount.

77. The lowminded man who, although he has knowledge (of the facts), declines to give his testimony, is, in sin, on a par with false witnesses; so is he, in his punishment.

78. In case of conflicting testimony, what is stated by the majority (of the witnesses) must be credited; if the numbers be equal, then those of the witnesses who are of distinguished qualities[159] must be credited; if again, these are in contradiction, then the most distinguished shall be credited.[160]

79. That party (to the suit) whose assertion the witnesses have verified, succeeds; that one whose assertion the witnesses have disproved, is defeated.

80. Although proof has been given by witnesses, yet, if others of more distinguished qualities or in number twice as many give opposite testimony, the first witnesses should be held as false ones.

81. As well they who suborn as they who give false testimony are to be severally fined in double the value of the suit:[161] a bráhman, in such case, shall be banished.[162]

82. [The witness] who, after he has been addressed[163] [by the judge, yet] being blinded by passion, withholds his testimony,—he shall pay eight times the [ordinary] fine: in case of a bráhman, he shall suffer banishment.[164]

---

sl. 232. To debauch a father's sister, or a mother's, the wife of a maternal uncle, a daughter-in-law, a step-mother, the sister or daughter of an *áchárya,*

sl. 233. or his wife, or one's own daughter,—these are equal to violation of a *guru's* bed. The penalty is death, the pudenda [of the criminal] being previously amputated. A like doom is for the woman, if she consented.

See Manu, ch. 9, sl. 235; ch. 11, sl. 54—58, sl. 170—180.

As to the *guru* and *áchárya,* the following is the 34th sloka of Yájnavalkya's first book:—He is a man's *guru,* who, after going through the ritual, imparts to him the Veda: he is *áchárya,* who invests with the sacred cord and then imparts the Veda.

[158] Manu, ch. 8, sl. 89 &c.

[159] *guni,* referring not merely to personal qualities or eminence in virtue, but to possession of wealth, sons, and learning: so explained by the Commentator.

[160] Manu, ch. 8, sl. 73.

[161] The Commentator explains this to refer to the fine which would be payable on failure (supra sl. 11).

[162] out of the realm. (*M.*) Manu, ch. 8. sl. 119-124.

[163] supra, sl. 73.

[164] The Commentator adds—If the bráhman, or any of the other casts, cannot pay the fine, he must suffer imprisonment and the labour proper to his cast. He explains the enor-

83. Should it happen that the testimony of a witness must occasion the death of a person, whatever the cast of the latter,—the witness shall, in such case, speak untruth.[165] For their purification [after giving such false testimony] the twice-born must make oblation to SARASWATI.[166]

84. If any settlement have been mutually come to [between debtor and creditor], a written instrument should be drawn up before witnesses, the first mention being of the creditor.

85. In it should be written the date, *viz.* year, month, half month, day, also the name, cast, family, the Veda-school, and father's name, of each party, &c.[167]

86. This being completed, the debtor shall subscribe with his signature [a declaration, as follows]:—"What is written above, I, the son of such an one, agree to."

87. Then the witnesses, all being equal in grade, shall, after their fathers' names, write, with their own hands respectively: "I, such an one, am a witness."

88. And the writer shall subscribe at the foot, as follows:—"This has been written, at the request of both parties, by me, such an one, the son of such an one."

89. An instrument, entirely in the handwriting of the party, is to be received as proof, although it be not witnessed, unless procured by violence or by fraud.[168]

90. Payment of a debt incurred upon a writing, is obligatory only upon the debtor, his son, and grand-son;[169] but a pledge shall remain in use so long as the debt is unpaid.

91. If the instrument be in a foreign country, be illegibly written, be destroyed, faded, stolen, mutilated, burned, or torn, [the Court] shall direct a new one to be made.

92. The authenticity of a written instrument which is doubtful, is to be ascertained by [comparison with other] documents in the handwriting of the party &c.,[170] by [enquiry into] the probability of its having been obtained,[171] and [the mode of] its preparation, by [observation of] any marks, by [enquiry of] the relation [in which the parties stand to each other], and how the matter came about.

93. As often as the debtor makes a payment, either he shall write an indorse-

---

mity of the offence described in this sloka to consist in the contempt of Court.

[165] *i. e.* if, by such untruth, the death be averted. If from testimony either way, the alternative of the death of the plaintiff or defendant must ensue, the witness should maintain silence, the monarch assenting. In case the monarch do not assent, the testimony may be rendered of no avail by confusing the witness: if this cannot be effected, then let the truth be spoken; for by so doing one fault only is incurred, *viz.* causing the death, whereas from untruth would arise the sin of it as well as of the death. (*M.*)

[166] Manu, ch. 8, sl. 104, 105.

[167] &c. *i. e.* his property, tribe, calling, customs, &c. (*M.*)

[168] Manu, ch. 8, sl. 168.

[169] literally "by three only," explained by the Commentator as above rendered.

[170] the Commentator considers the &c. here to signify, testing the handwriting of the writers or amanuenses employed.

[171] *i. e.* consideration of place, time, and persons connected with possession of the document. (*M.*)

ment to that effect on the document, or the creditor shall give a receipt under his hand.

94. When the debt is paid, [the debtor] shall cause the document to be torn up, or shall have another prepared, *viz.* of discharge. If the debt was incurred before witnesses, its payment should also be before witnesses.[172]

95. The scales, fire, water, poison, the sacred draught—these are the ordeals for exculpation,[173] in case of grave accusations, if the accuser be prepared to pay a fine.

96. When it is agreed on; one of the parties shall perform [the ordeal], the other be in readiness to pay the fine. Even without a fine, there shall be trial by ordeal in case of treason or great crime.

97. [The accused,] being summoned, shall, after bathing at sunrise and fasting, be made to go through the several ordeals, in presence of the monarch and the bráhmans.

98. The scales are [the ordeal] for women, children, aged men, the blind, the lame, bráhmans, and those afflicted with disease. Fire or water, or the seven barleycorns' weight of poison are [the ordeal] for a Śúdrá.

99. For a less value than a thousand *panas*, one shall not go through the ordeal of the [heated] iron plough-share, of poison, or of the scales: but in case of offence against the monarch or great crime, purifications[174] shall always be gone through.

100. When the accused has been placed in the scales by those who understand the art of weighing, a counter-weight adjusted, and a line drawn, he is then to be taken out [of the scales.]

101. "O scales! made by the gods, of old, the abode of truth: therefore do ye, propitious ones, declare the truth and liberate me from suspicion!

102. If I be an evil-doer, then bear me down, oh mother! If I be pure, carry me upwards!" Thus shall he [who is to go through the ordeal] invoke the scales.

103. The hands [of the accused] shall be inspected when rice has been rubbed in them; after which, seven leaves of the Indian fig tree are to be placed therein

[172] The Commentator divides written instruments into, 1. public or given by authority, and, 2. private, or those which the community use among themselves, and to which the rules in the text apply. These again are either, autograph, *i. e.* wholly written by the party who speaks by the document—or, written by another for him. The last description, he says, require to be attested, and their effect as proof depends upon local usage. He quotes Nárada as to the private writings. For the instruments emanating from authority, he refers to sl. 317, 318, 319 of Yájnavalkya's first Book, *viz.*

"When the monarch bestows lands or creates a charge in favor of any one, he shall, for information of future good monarchs, put it in writing, either on cloth or copper, setting his seal thereto. He shall inscribe the names of his ancestors and his own [also the donee's (*M.*)], the extent of the gift, its description by boundaries, also the date; all this shall be authenticated under his hand."

[173] This word in the 94th sloka we have rendered 'discharge.' Its ordinary and literal sense is 'purification.'

[174] *scil.* ordeals. (*M.*)

[*scil.* in his hands] and fastened round successively with a thread.

104. "Thou, O fire, dwellest in all created things! O purifier, in testimony of innocence and guilt, do thou, in my hand, make known the truth!"

105. When he [who suffers the ordeal] has thus spoken, let a smooth red hot iron ball, of fifty *palas* weight, be placed upon both his hands.

106. Carrying this, let him slowly walk across seven circles, of sixteen fingers breadth diameter each, with an interval of the same measure between each.

107. If, having thrown down the fireball, and being [again] rubbed with rice, he [the accused] is unburnt, his purification is accomplished. Should the ball during [the trial] fall down, or should there be any doubt, he is to take [it] again.

108. "By the power of truth, O Varuṇa,[175] save me!" Thus invoking the water, and grasping the thighs of a man standing in water up to his navel, let him [who goes through this ordeal] submerge himself.

109. An arrow at the same instant shot [from the bow] a swift footed-man shall [run and] fetch: should he, upon his return, see that the body [of the accused] is still submerged, the latter is to be exculpated.

110. "Thou, O poison, Bráhmá's[176] son, art ordained for truth and right; free me from the accusation, and be to me, by the power of truth, a draught of immortality!"

111. Thus speaking, he shall eat of poison produced by the Sringa tree, of the Himálaya. Whoever is able to digest this without evil effect, shall be declared innocent.

112. Let the judge, adoring terrible deities, and taking of the water in which [their images] have been bathed, adjure it, and cause [the accused] to drink off three times the contents of his palms.

113. He to whom, within fourteen days from this [ordeal], no great calamity happens, either from the monarch or by act of God, shall without doubt be [held] guiltless.

114. A father when making partition [of his property], can divide it among his sons as he pleases; either giving to the eldest the best share or in such wise that all share equally.[177]

115. If he give equal shares, such of his wives as have not received *stridhana* from their husband or father-in-law shall also equally share.[178]

116. If one have means, and do not desire [to share in the paternal estate], he

---

[175] the ocean god.

[176] the inferior Brahmá, the immediate cause or creator of the universe.

[177] It is only of self-acquired property that unequal partition can be made. Of that which is inherited or ancestral, there is co-ownership: it cannot therefore be apportioned at the father's pleasure. (*M.*) Infra sl. 121.

[178] Jagannát'ha, in his Digest, quotes the Dipakaliká and other authorities interpreting this injunction to refer to such wives only as have not male issue. (Colebrooke, vol. 3, p. 97.)

shall be separated, something trifling being given to him.[179] A distribution by a father in smaller or larger shares, if in accordance with the Sástras, is lawful.[180]

117. After decease of the parents, let the sons make equal division of the property and of the debts.[181] And so the daughters, of what is left of the mother's [*stridhana*], after [paying] her debts; and, if there be no daughters, the sons or others of the family [being heirs, take it].

118. What has been self-acquired by any one, as an increment, without diminishing the paternal estate, likewise a gift from a friend or a marriage-gift, does not belong to the coheirs.[182]

119. If one have recovered ancestral property which had been purloined, he has not to give it up to the coheirs;[183] nor shall a man share the earnings of science.[184]

120. If however the common property be augmented, equal division is enjoined.[185] In making division among several grandsons, regard should be had to the respective [portions of their deceased] fathers;

121. inasmuch as the ownership of father and son is co-equal in the acquisitions of the grandfather, whether land, any settled income, or moveables.

122. If a son be born of a wife of equal cast, after partition made, he is to share; or a share may be allotted him from the estate as it is, after allowing for income

---

[179] Something, however valueless; in order that the heirs of the separated son may have no claim to a share of the family inheritance, (*M.*) Manu, ch. 9, sl. 207.

[180] For instance, if one son have a large family, or be disqualified to earn a livelihood, the father may give him a portion larger than the others. But an unequal partition from angry impulse, or weak-mindedness, has no validity. (*M.*)

[181] Manu, ch. 9, sl. 104. Whenever the father wishes, is one of the ordained periods for partition; the second is, when the father has renounced worldly enjoyment and the mother is past child-bearing; and this partition may be enforced (according to Nárada) at the son's desire, though the father object. Partition should also be made, the son desiring it, if the father lead a vicious life, or be suffering under incurable disease; even though the mother's menstruation have not ceased. The third period for partition is, the father's decease. (*M.*) Manu divides,—to the eldest two aliquot parts, to the second son one and a half, and to each succeeding son a single part. The Commentator asks, why that division was not adhered to; and he solves his own question by the remark, that it was disliked by the people, and therefore rightly abandoned. This position he supports by several quotations, and by allusion to the abolition or non-observance of other ancient ordinances, *e.g.* the raising up of male heirs by the brother of the husband or others.

It is an obvious reflection, that the altered law of distribution is one of the few instances in the Hindu economy where an innate feeling of natural equality has overcome or superseded arbitrary rule—and further, that the change has been brought about by the pressure of the old law upon the privileged casts, who, in common with others, were affected by it.

[182] Manu, ch. 9, sl. 206, 208.

[183] When the recovered properly is land, he who obtained it shall take a fourth part, the remainder to be equally divided. (*M.*) The Commentator supports this view by the authority of Sankha. Manu, ch. 9, sl. 209.

[184] Supra, Book 1, sl. 3.

[185] Manu, ch. 9, sl. 215.

and expenditure.[186]

123. Whatever property may be given by the parents to any child, shall belong to that child. If partition be made after the father's death, the mother shall also have an equal share.[187]

124. Those of the brothers whose ritual ceremonies have not been accomplished, shall have them completed by the others whose ritual is gone through: so in like manner as to the ritual of sisters, [each of the brethren] devoting a fourth part of his share.[188]

125. The sons of a bráhman, shall receive, according to their [mother's] cast, four parts, or three, or two, or one: the sons of a kshattriya [in like manner], three, or two, or one: and the sons of a vaisyá, two, or one.[189]

126. Whatever, after partition has taken place, may be discovered to have been wrongly appropriated by one of the sharers,[190] shall be equally divided among them all: this is enjoined.

127. A son begotten by one who is without male issue, in obedience to precept,[191] upon another man's wife, becomes by law heir to both, and presents the death-oblations of both.[192]

128. (I) "An *aurasa*[193] son," is one born of a *dharma*[194] wife; equal with him is

---

[186] The Commentator refers, in explanation of this sloka, to Manu, ch. 9, sl. 216, *viz.* A son born after a division shall alone inherit the patrimony [*i. e.* the share allotted to the parents (*M.*)], or shall have a share of it with the divided brethren, if they return and unite themselves with him.—With respect to the deduction for expenditure, &c., the Commentator explains, that the accumulations of mere income are not to be included in the estate to be repartitioned, and that a previous deduction is to be made for necessary expenditure, *e.g.* the father's debts.

[187] but, if she have *stridhana*, only a half share. (*M.*)

[188] Manu, ch. 9, sl. 118.

[189] These varying proportions ofcourse apply only where there are several mothers of differing casts. Manu, ch. 9, sl. 148-157.

[190] or escaped notice altogether. (*M.*) Manu, ch. 9, sl. 218.

[191] Manu, ch. 9, sl. 59, 145, 167, 190.

[192] But if the actual father have already a son, his son by another's wife is not his heir. (*M.*)

[193] *aurasa* is from *úras* 'the best,' being the first in order of sons.

[194] *dharma* wife is defined by the Commentator, a wife of the same cast with her husband, and wedded to him according to the *bráhma* and other approved forms of marriage; which are described in the first book, sl. 58-61, *viz.* "In the marriage called *bráhma*, [the bride], adorned in a manner suitable to the means [of her family], is bestowed upon the invited bridegroom,—In the *daiva* [marriage, the bride is made over] to the priest whilst offering sacrifice: *ársha* [marriage], is where [the bride's father] receives a pair of kine.—In the *káya* [marriage, the bride] is delivered to the suitor with the injunction, Together practise the rules of duty! In the *asura* [marriage], wealth is received [from the bridegroom]. *Gándharva* is [a union in marriage] by mutual consent [of the parties]: the *rákshasa* [marriage], is by capture [of the woman] in war: the *paisácha* [marriage, where she is obtained] by deception." Manu ch. 3, sl. 20 *et. seq.*

(II) "A daughter's son."[195]

(III) "A wife's son," is a son begotten by

a relative[196] [of the husband] or by another [duly authorised].

129 (iv) "A son of hidden birth," is one brought forth in private, in the [husband's] dwelling.[197]

(v) "A girl's son," is one born of an unmarried girl;[198] he is considered the son of the maternal grandfather.

130 (vi) "A son of the twice-married," is one born of a woman [by a second marriage], whether she be [at the time of that marriage] a maid or not.[199]

(vii) "A son by gift," is one who is made a gift of, either by his father or his mother.[200]

131 (viii) "A son by purchase," is one sold by his parents.[201]

(ix) "A son made," is a son [born of parents deceased,] selected by any one for himself.

(x) "A self-given son," is one who has given himself [as a son to another.][202]

(xi) "A son with the bride," is one of whom the mother is already pregnant [by another than her husband] when she marries.[203]

132 (xii) "A deserted son," is one adopted upon being forsaken [by his own parents.[204]]

The first in order that there may be, of the sons above described, shall present the oblation cake[205] and take the inheritance.[206]

---

[195] *scil.* according to Vaśishṭha, such as, by agreement between father and son-in-law, at the time of the daughter's marriage, has been, by anticipation, given up to the father. (*M.*) And the Commentator notes, that the term used, *puttrikásata*, may be also rendered or understood 'daughter as a son' *i. e.* a daughter appointed or placed in the same position and with the same rights as a son.

[196] *sagotra.*

[197] it being merely known that the father is a man of the same cast, not who he is. (*M.*)

[198] privately, in the father's house. (*M.*) Manu adds the condition, if she marry her lover; ch. 9, sl. 172.

[199] Manu, ch. 9, sl. 175.

[200] This is permitted to a man of the same cast, in time of distress; but only where there are several sons: the eldest cannot be bestowed as a gift-son. (*M.*) Manu, ch. 9, sl. 168.

[201] The Commentator explains, that this can only be on the same conditions as the given or gift son. Manu, ch. 9, sl. 174.

[202] having lost his parents, or being abandoned by them. (*M.*) We have some doubt of the Commentator's meaning: here as the alternative includes a separate head and description, *viz.* (xii) in the succeeding sloka. The word rendered 'abandoned' literally signifies 'liberated,' 'set free;' so the meaning may be, — one who is left free to choose for himself.

[203] Manu, ch. 9, sl. 173.

[204] ibid. sl. 171.

[205] *piṇḍa*, which literally signifies any round substance. The cake is a compound, in form of a ball, given as an offering to the dead.

[206] The Commentator quotes Vaśishṭha—If a son be adopted, and afterwards an *aura-*

133. Such is the rule enjoined by me for sons where there is equality of cast. Even the son begotten by a Śúdrá, on a slave-woman, shall have such share as [the father] may allot.[207]

134. [But if there be no partition till] after the father's death, then the brothers [born in marriage] are to assign him half a share: if there be no brothers nor daughters' sons, he then takes the whole.

135, 136. If a man depart this life without male issue; (i) his wife, (ii) his daughters, (iii) his parents,[208] (iv) his brothers,[209] (v) the sons of brothers,[210] (vi) others of the same *gotra*,[211] (vii) kindred more remote,[212] (viii) a pupil, (ix) a fellow-student[213]—these succeed to the inheritance; each class upon failure of the one preceding. This rule applies to all the casts.

137. The heirs of a hermit, of a religious ascetic, of a professed *brahmachári*,[214] are successively, the preceptor, the disciple, and an associate dwelling in the same religious retreat.

sa be born, the former takes a fourth part—and deduces from this, that a son of any inferior grade receives a fourth share when superseded by an afterborn *aurasa*.

[207] Manu, ch. 9, sl. 179.

[208] *pitárau*. First the mother, then the father—says the Commentator. But Manu, ch. 9, sl. 185:—If a man die without male issue, the father is heir; next to him in order, the brothers—and, sl. 217—If a man die childless, his mother succeeds.—Such is the contradictory character of texts and comments on this subject. The law in use in Bengal is the reverse of the Commentator's gloss.

[209] first, of the whole blood; then, half-brothers. (*M.*)

[210] as representing their respective fathers. (*M.*)

[211] family; kindred of the same *stirpes* or stock. These are thus detailed by the Commentator;

     1. paternal grandmother,
     2. paternal grandfather,
     3. paternal uncles,
     4. sons of the uncles,

on failure of paternal grandfather's line, then,

     5. paternal great-grandmother,
     6. paternal great-grandfather,
     7. their sons,
     8. their sons' offspring.

All of whom (proceeds the Commentator) are *sapindas*, connected by food oblations. If they fail, then follow those connected by the water oblation only, *viz.* seven degrees in the ascending line beyond *sapindas*, *i. e. samánodacas*.

[212] divided by the Commentator into three classes, *viz.*

1. of one's self, 2. of one's father, 3. of one's mother; as, the sons of a father's or of a mother's sister, or a maternal uncle (one's own kin)—the sons of a father's paternal or maternal aunt, or a father's maternal uncle (a father's kin)—and those in the same relation to a mother.

[213] *sa-brahmachári*, one instructed together with him in his religious duties. This head applies only to the first three classes, those invested with the sacred cord.

[214] as distinguished from the temporary *brahmachári* or religious student, which all of the twice born classes should be, in youth.

138. One reunited[215] shall take the portion of his deceased reunited co-sharer, and shall give it up to a [son, if one be afterwards] born.[216] This is always so with uterine brothers.

139. A reunited half-brother shall take the property; not a [separated] half-brother: but a [uterine brother] whether reunited or not, shall take; this not being so with the half-brother.[217]

140. An impotent, an outcast as well as his son,[218] a cripple, a madman, an idiot, one blind, one incurably diseased, and such like,[219] are to be maintained, but do not share in the inheritance.

141. The *aurasa* sons of those [disqualified] persons, also their wives' sons,[220] if themselves free from defect,[221] succeed to shares; and their daughters[222] are to be maintained until provided with husbands.

142. [So] their childless wives shall be maintained, if of good conduct; but shall be cast off, if of vicious habits, or of an evil nature.[223]

143. What has been given [to a woman] by her father, her mother, her husband, or her brother, or received by her before the nuptial fire, or on occasion of her husband's marriage with another wife, and such like,[224] is called *stridhana*.

144. Gifts from her kindred, from the bridegroom [before marriage], also subsequent gifts, descend to her own kindred, should she die without issue.

145. The *stridhana* of a wife dying without issue, who has been married in one of the four forms of marriage designated *bráhma* &c.,[225] belongs to the husband;

---

[215] who, having been separated, again holds his property in community with those from whom he had separated. Such reunion is permitted only with the father, the brothers, and the paternal uncle. (*M.*)

[216] This participle has a masculine termination; and the ellipsis is supplied from the Commentator.

[217] This is rather the paraphrase of the Commentator: the text is very obscure. Yájnavalkya in these two verses promulgates, according to the Commentator, the following law. A wife or a daughter or a mother shall not be entitled (under a preceding rule) to take the heritage, when there has been a reunion, after separation, of male members of the family; and of course where there has been no division. In the case of united brothers, where there is a full brother in the union, he takes the property, in preference to a half-brother; but, if the half-brother be united and the full brother separate, the two will divide the property between them. When, of many full brothers, some live united and others separate, those united will have the preference. If there be half brothers, as well as full brothers, in the union, the former take nothing; but all full brothers, living separate, share with one or more united half-brothers. Where the brothers all live separate the rule will of course not apply.

[218] *i. e.* according to the Ratnákara, a son born after his degradation from cast.

[219] *scil.* hermits, devotees, one who is his father's enemy, one guilty of a crime of minor degree, one deaf or dumb, one deprived of an organ of sense. (*M.*)

[220] supra sl. 128 (III).

[221] such as described sl. 140. (*M.*)

[222] if there be no sons. (*M.*)

[223] These three slokas are analogous to Manu, ch. 9, sl. 201, 2, 3.

[224] *scil.* acquisitions by inheritance, purchase, partition, gift, finding. (*M.*)

[225] supra, note[**].

if she have issue, then the *stridhana* goes to her daughters; should she have been married in another form,[226] then her *stridhana* goes to her parents.[227]

146. Whoso withholds his daughter,[228] after having promised to give her [in marriage], shall be amerced, and shall reimburse all expenses incurred with interest. If she die [after being affianced] he [*i. e.* the bridegroom] shall receive back what he has given, deduction being made for the expenditure on both sides.

147. A husband need not return to his wife *stridhana* appropriated by him, during a famine, or in order to perform sacred rites,[229] or when suffering from disease,[230] or when in prison.[231]

148. If he marry another wife, he shall give to the one he has, as a consideration for superseding her, should she not already have received *stridhana*, what is equivalent [to his gifts on the second marriage]: but, should she have already received *stridhana*, then, it is declared, [she is entitled to only] half the amount.[232]

149. If the fact of a partition be denied, the matter shall be ascertained by [reference to] relatives, near or remote, witnesses, and writings, also [by enquiry as to] separate possession of messuage and land.[233]

150. When there is a dispute as to boundaries, the neighbours of the [disputed] land, old men and the like,[234] cowherds, cultivators of the soil close to the [disputed] boundary, and all whose business is in forests —[235]

151. —these shall determine the boundaries, as they are indicated by elevated ground, by charcoal [-remnants],[236] by husks,[237] by trees, by a causeway, by anthills, by depressions of the soil, by bones, by memorials,[238] and such like.[239]

152. Otherwise,[240] four, eight, or ten neighbours of the same village, wearing a red wreath and red garments, and carrying earth, shall settle the boundary.[241]

---

[226] *asura, gándarbha, rákshasa, paiśácha.*

[227] *i. e.* if she die without issue. (*M.*)

[228] without just cause. (*M.*) Yájnavalkya himself suggests as a sufficient cause, a more eligible bridegroom offering; B. 1, sl. 65.

[229] if he have no other means. (*M.*)

[230] if he have no other means. (*M.*)

[231] if he have no other means. (*M.*)

[232] The Commentator and other authorities interpret *arddha* in this place to signify, such proportionate part as shall make the entire *stridhana* of the first wife equal to that of the second.

[233] and further, by enquiry as to the mode of performing religious rites in the family. (*M.*)

[234] Explained by the Commentator such as are free (as aged men are presumed to be) from the trammels of worldly occupation and of passion.

[235] Manu, ch. 8, sl. 258—262.

[236] the remains of burnt fuel. (*M.*)

[237] of rice. (*M.*)

[238] stones or other landmarks. (*M.*)

[239] Manu, ch. 8, sl. 246—252.

[240] *i. e.* if none of the means indicated in the previous sloka are available. (*M.*)

[241] Manu, ch. 8, sl. 254—258.

153. And if any falsehood be uttered, upon each one [speaking falsely] the monarch shall impose the medium fine.[242]

In the absence of any persons having knowledge of the matter, and of any indicatory signs, the monarch shall mark the boundary.[243]

154. The same rule applies to fruit-gardens, to out-houses, to villages,[244] to wells or tanks, to pleasure-gardens, and to dwellings, as well as to watercourses caused by the rain.[245]

155. If the boundary be broken, or be overstepped,[246] if a field[247] be taken away; the lowest, the highest and the medium fines shall be imposed.[248]

156. [Constructing] a useful dam, if it occasion but slight damage [to individuals], is not to be prevented; nor is a well[249] which takes from another's land, if having an abundant supply of water and not of large extent.

157. If one construct a dam in a field, without notice to the owner thereof, the right to use it, when complete, shall belong to the owner of the field: if the field be without owner, then the user belongs to the monarch.

158. Whoso fails to complete the cultivation of a field which he has partially ploughed, shall be made to pay [to the landowner] the value of the [expected] crop. He[250] shall complete the cultivation by means of another.

159. If a female buffalo spoil corn,[251] [her owner] shall be fined eight *máshas*,[252] if a cow, the half [of that sum]; if a goat or a sheep, the half of the latter.

160. If, after having grazed, they repose there, the fine shall be double what is above specified.

The same [rule applies] to land kept for pasture. An ass and a camel are [in this respect] the same as a female buffalo.

161. There shall be an indemnity for the owner of the field equal in value to the corn destroyed.[253] The herdsmen shall receive a beating, but the cattle-owner be punished by fine, as before mentioned.

---

[242] ibid, sl. 263.

[243] ibid, sl. 265.

[244] and towns. (*M.*)

[245] Manu, ch. 8, sl. 262.

[246] The Commentator describes a boundary as a strip or border (a party-ridge) of land, used in common. The breaking therefore must mean some material alteration of this border. Overstepping, the Commentator describes to be cultivating beyond the boundary.

[247] or house or garden, &c. (*M.*)

[248] *scil.* reddendo singula singulis, the lowest fine for breaking, the highest for overstepping, the medium for wrongful appropriation. Manu, ch. 8, sl. 264; ch. 9, sl. 291.

[249] or similar constructions, as a tank, &c. (*M.*)

[250] *semble*, the landowner. The Commentator throws no light on this ambiguity.

[251] or any other crop. (*M.*)

[252] a *másha* is the twentieth part of a copper *pana*. (*M.*) Supra pa. 7.

[253] Manu, ch. 8, sl. 241.

162. No guilt attaches[254] [to the cattle-owner,] if the field[255] be close to the public road, or to the village pasture lands,[256] and he do not intend [the trespass]; if he do intend it, then he incurs punishment as a thief.

163. A bull, cattle permitted to be at large,[257] a cow that has recently calved, estrays,[258] and the like,[259] having no keeper or brought there by accident or by act of the monarch, shall be let go free.[260]

164. The herdsman shall, at the close of the day, give back the cattle, in the same manner[261] as they were delivered to him: if he be in receipt of wages, he shall replace such as have, through his negligence, died or been lost.[262]

165. If loss accrue by fault of the herdsman, he shall be fined thirteen *paṇas* and a half, and shall make good the loss to the owner.

166. Pasture-ground shall be allotted for cattle, such as the villagers agree upon, or in proportion to the whole area of land, or as the monarch wills.

A twice-born man may, in every place, appropriate as his own, grass, fuel, and flowers.[263]

167. There shall be a space of one hundred *dhanus*[264] between a *gráma*,[265] and the [surrounding] fields, of two hundred for a *karvaṭa*,[266] of four hundred for a *nagara*.[267]

168. A man may seize any thing, belonging to himself, which another has sold.[268] The purchaser incurs blame, if [he have bought] secretly: and, if [he bought] from a low man,[269] with secrecy, for a small price, and at an unusual

---

[254] no penalty therefore or liability. (*M.*)

[255] being an open field. (*M.*)

[256] Manu, ch. 8, sl. 237, 8, 9.

[257] let loose to propitiate the gods. (*M.*)

[258] wanderers from a distant herd. (*M.*)

[259] *scil.* other animals, as elephants, horses, &c. (*M.*)

[260] Manu, ch. 8, sl. 242.

[261] *i. e.* counting them. (*M.*)

[262] Manu, ch. 8, sl. 232.

[263] for oblations to the gods. (*M.*) Manu does not expressly restrict this privilege to the twice-born; ch. 8, sl. 339.

[264] This term (literally 'a bow') is a land measure, equivalent to the modern oottah or four hâts.

[265] These three are in progressive increase: the first is, a mere village; the second, the central or sudder station of several villages; the third, a town of more extended population and importance. Manu, ch. 8, sl. 237.

[266] These three are in progressive increase: the first is, a mere village; the second, the central or sudder station of several villages; the third, a town of more extended population and importance. Manu, ch. 8, sl. 237.

[267] These three are in progressive increase: the first is, a mere village; the second, the central or sudder station of several villages; the third, a town of more extended population and importance. Manu, ch. 8, sl. 237.

[268] or which has been given away, or pledged, by a stranger without right. (*M.*) Manu, ch. 8, sl. 199.

[269] *scil.* one destitute of property. (*M.*) The expression in the text is applicable to any

hour, he is [to be accounted] a thief.

169. If one obtain property [which he afterwards discovers to have been] lost or stolen, he should cause the taker[270] of it to be secured: should time or the place not permit of this being done, he must himself restore the property [to its owner].

170. Upon his producing the seller, he [the possessor,] is himself cleared: the owner takes the property, the monarch the fine, and the [defrauded] purchaser the value from the seller.

171. [A claim to] property [as] lost,[271] is to be supported by proof of acquisition[272] or of user: [the claimant,] if he fail, shall pay to the monarch one-fifth of the value [of the property] as a fine.

172. Whoever takes [back] from the hand of a stranger what has been stolen or lost [from himself] without informing the monarch, shall pay a fine of ninety six *paṇas*.[273]

173. When lost or stolen property has been recovered by customs officers or by the local police, the owner may claim it until one year has elapsed;[274] after that time it goes to the monarch.

174. If it be a single-hoofed animal, the owner shall pay four *paṇas*; if a man, five *paṇas*; if a buffalo, or a camel, or a cow, two *paṇas*; if a goat or a sheep, the fourth part of a *paṇa*.[275]

175.[276]Any property, other than women and children, may be given away, if it be no detriment to the family—but not the whole property, where there are children; nor any portion which has been already promised to another.

176. The acceptance [of a gift] should be public, especially of immovable property. Whatever may be lawfully given and is contracted to be given, shall not, after gift, be resumed.

177. The time given for trial [on purchase] of seed, is ten days;[277] of iron, one day; of beasts of burden, five days; of precious stones, seven days; of women,[278] one month; of milch-cows, three days; of men,[279] half a month.

---

whose position or lack of means might justify a suspicion that he had not come honestly by the goods.

[270] the man who sold or assigned it to him. (*M.*)

[271] or stolen, or given in pledge. (*M.*)

[272] Supra, sl. 27.

[273] Inasmuch as he abets concealment of the thief or wrongdoer. (*M.*)

[274] Manu, ch. 8, sl. 30. The Commentator accounts for the discrepancy between the two law-givers by supposing Manu to have alluded to the property of learned bráhmaṇs only.

[275] This fine is considered by the Commentator a consideration or indemnity for safe keeping, and an exception to the rule laid down by Manu, ch. 8, sec. 33.

[276] Colebrooke's rendering of this sloka (Digest ch. 4, sec. 1, §16,) differs from ours, which however we consider to be the correct signification of the text before us.

[277] Manu, ch. 8, sl. 222.

[278] The Commentator explains this to refer to slaves.

[279] The Commentator explains this to refer to slaves.

178. By the action of fire, gold is not lessened in quantity: one hundred *palas*[280] of silver thereby lose two *palas*; of tin, one hundred *palas* lose eight; lead and copper, out of one hundred *palas*, lose five; iron, of one hundred *palas*, loses ten.[281]

179. One hundred *palas* of wool or cotton when worked[282] are increased by ten *palas*; if the thread be of middling fineness, the increase is five *palas*; if very fine, three *palas*.

180. In figured textures and in those made of hair, the loss is estimated at one thirtieth part. In a texture of silk or of the bark of trees, there is neither loss nor increase.

181. Whenever loss has been sustained, the artisan shall be imperatively required to pay what competent judges award, after they shall have investigated [circumstances, of] place, of time, of the mode of using [the material], and its quality of strength or lightness.[283]

182. One made a slave by compulsion, and one sold[284] [into slavery] by robbers, are [entitled to be] set free; so also is [a slave] who saves his master's life; also one who [having adopted servitude for a living,] abandons his claim to maintenance; also one enslaved who pays off what is due from him.[285]

183. One who, being a religious mendicant, forsakes that condition, shall be, until death, the monarch's slave. Slavery must be in the order of the casts, not inversely.[286]

184. Though an apprentice have attained a knowledge of his art,[287] he shall [nevertheless] remain in his master's house for the stipulated time, receiving from his master maintenance, and giving up to him his earnings.[288]

[280] Supra, p. 7.

[281] These facts are related, says the Commentator, as an index to or test of the honesty of metal-workers.

[282] Made into coarse thread. (*M.*)

[283] This sloka, as appears from the Commentary, is in allusion to the loss on working or manufacture of textile fabrics mentioned in the previous slokas.

[284] or given or pledged. (*M.*)

[285] The slavery or servitude being to secure or work out a debt.

[286] *e.g.* a bráhmaṇ cannot be slave to a kshattriya. Manu, ch. 8, sl. 410–15.

[287] *scil.* medicine or handicraft. (*M.*)

[288] The Commentator thus explains and analyses the subject of servitude or working for others:

There are two descriptions of persons who serve. I. Those whose employment is of a respectable kind. II. Those whose employment is not so. The first division he subdivides into—1, the disciple; 2, the apprentice; 3, the workman; 4, the overseer.

The disciple is the student of the vedas; the apprentice is one learning an art; the workman is one who is paid for his work; the overseer superintends workmen. There are three sorts of workmen—1, soldiers; 2, husbandmen; 3, they who bear burdens.

II. The other and meaner description of employment is performed by slaves, *scil.* cleaning the house, cleaning away filth, &c.

Slaves, the Commentator subdivides, according to their origin and mode of enslavement, into fifteen classes, *scil.*

185. The monarch shall erect in the city a mansion and shall settle therein bráhmans learned in the three Vedas, and endow them, giving them injunction to discharge their duties.[289]

186. They shall diligently practise all observances stipulated for[290] [in the endowment] which do not interfere with their personal duties, also whatever other observances the monarch may enjoin.[291]

187. Whoso appropriates what belongs to the community or violates his engagement [with the community], shall forfeit his property and be banished the realm.[292]

188. The word of those who [are appointed to] superintend the affairs[293] of the community must be obeyed by all [the members]: he who acts in violation thereof shall be amerced in the first [i. e. lowest] fine.[294]

189. Those who have come [from other parts] upon the affairs of the community shall, upon completion of the business, be dismissed by the monarch, with gifts, with honour, and with hospitable entertainment.

190. An emissary upon the business of the community shall deliver up whatever he has received [on their account]: if he fail to deliver voluntarily, he shall be amerced eleven times the value [of what he withholds].

191. They who have direction of the affairs of the community should be such as know their duties,[295] are pure minded, and not covetous; their word for the welfare of the community is to be followed.

    1. A born slave of the house.
    2. A purchased slave.
    3. One [otherwise] acquired *e.g.* by donation.
    4. One obtained by inheritance.
    5. One rescued from starvation during a famine.
    6. One received in pledge.
    7. One who becomes a slave to discharge a debt.
    8. A captive in war.
    9. One whose freedom has been lost by wager.
    10. A volunteer slave.
    11. An apostate from the condition of a *pravajita* or religious mendicant.
    12. A slave for a prescribed term.
    13. A slave for subsistence sake.
    14. One enslaved by espousing a woman who is a slave.
    15. One who has sold himself.

[289] *scil.* duties prescribed by the Śruti and Smriti, according to their cast and grade. (*M.*)

[290] such as, tending cattle, conservation of water, care of temples, &c. (*M.*)

[291] *scil.* to entertain travellers, or injunction to see that horses or other provision be not furnished to the enemies of the State. (*M.*)

[292] *i. e.* for a heinous offence: for minor offences, fines, as declared by Manu, shall be imposed. (*M.*) Manu, ch. 8, sl. 220, is probably here referred to.

[293] The term used *hitavádi* signifies, who speak for the welfare of; which we assume to have the sense we have given to it.

[294] Supra bk. 1, sl. 365.

[295] Supra note[††].

192. What has just been enjoined is obligatory in like manner upon communities of craftsmen, of traders, and of *páshaṇḍas*.[296] The monarch should preserve their distinctive character, and make them respectively adhere to their original callings.[297]

193. If one, after receipt of wages, abandon his work, he shall pay double the amount; if [he desert] when he has not received [his wages], he shall pay a sum equal [to his wages].[298]

The implements shall be in charge of the workman.[299]

194. The monarch shall oblige him who gets work done without having previously fixed the rate of hire, to pay a tenth part, [whether] earnings in trade or [in care] of cattle, or [in cultivation] of corn.

195. A master[300] may treat as he thinks right one who disregards time or place, or [so acts that he] prevents profit being earned.[301]

The more that is done, the more shall be given.

196. Where work [contracted for by two] cannot be proceeded with by the two,[302] [the one who has to abandon the work] shall be paid according to what he has performed; but, if practicable, the original contract should be carried out.[303]

197. If goods [when in transport from place to place] be lost, the carrier shall pay their value; except [the loss be] occasioned by the monarch or by act of God. If he [who has contracted to transport goods] cause them not to start on the journey, he shall be made to pay twice the amount of his hire:

198. if he abandon [his charge] when at the outset of the journey, he shall pay [a sum equal to] a seventh part [of the hire]; if, when he has proceeded to some distance, a fourth part; if when half-way, the entire amount of hire. The like [rule is to be observed] where [the hirer] breaks [his contract].

199. If a professed gambler win at play [as much as] one hundred [*paṇas*], he shall pay to the keeper of the house one-fifth: others shall pay [the keeper] a tenth of their winnings.

200. The latter,[304] [in consideration of] having [royal] protection, shall pay the portion stipulated to the monarch, shall make over all stakes won to the winner, shall be true of speech, and forbearing.

---

[296] Lassen, in his *Indische Alterthumskunde* (vol. 2, p. 238), speaking of the edicts of king Asoca (B. C. 250), which refer to *páshaṇḍas*, describes these as a sect who disbelieved alike in the bráhmiṇical and buddhist tenets. We have, in sloka 70, rendered the word 'infidels.'

[297] Manu, ch. 8, sl. 41, 219, 21, 410, 18.

[298] ibid. sl. 215—218.

[299] The expression is 'servant,' as opposed to, master, or employer.

[300] *scil.* a merchant, owner of cattle, or landed proprietor. (*M.*)

[301] As, by improvident expenditure. (*M.*)

[302] Signifying plurality generally. (*M.*)

[303] Colebrooke renders this sloka differently; Dig. B. 3, ch. 1, sec. 1, §65. We have adhered closely to the text.

[304] *scil.* the keeper.

201. The monarch shall enforce payment of winnings; [that is,] such as are made in a place kept by a licensed gaming-house-master paying the royal dues, among known players, meeting openly; in other cases, not.

202. They who manage suits [arising out of the games], also the witnesses, are to be such persons as those last described.

If any one play with false dice or cheat, the monarch shall have him branded and banished.

203. An overseer of the games should be appointed, who may thus become familiar with [the persons of reputed] thieves.[305]

The like rules apply to wagers at fighting games, whether of men or brutes.[306]

204. If any give abusive words to one deprived of a limb or an organ of sense, or diseased, whether the words be true or untrue, or [in the guise of] ironical praise,—he shall be fined thirteen *panas* and a half.[307]

205. The monarch shall compel one who uses such insulting language as, "I will go to thy sister" or "to thy mother,"[308] to pay a fine of twenty-five *panas*.

206. Half [of this fine is to be imposed when the offensive words are] to inferiors, double if to the wives of other men or to superiors. The fine shall be regulated according to the higher or lower cast of the parties.[309]

207. [Thus;] if the offence occurs, [where the parties are] in the ascending line of cast, the fine shall be double or treble [as may be]; if in the descending line, the fine shall be always lessened one half.[310]

208. If injury be threatened to a person's arm, or neck or eyes or thigh, the fine shall be one hundred *panas*; if to the foot or nose or ear or hand, and the like,[311] half of that [fine].

209. If the threat be by one who has not the power [to carry out his threat], he shall be fined ten *panas*; [the threatener] who has the power shall be, in addition, compelled to give surety for the safety of the person [threatened].

210. For abuse by imputation of a crime which would entail loss of cast, the middle fine [shall be exacted]; if of a lesser crime, the lowest fine.

211. If the abuse be directed against one conversant with the three Vedas, against the monarch, or against the gods, the highest fine [is incurred]; if against a whole cast or a community, the middle fine; if against a village or the realm, the

[305] Infra sl. 267.

[306] But one word is used in the original, which the Commentator thus explains. The foregoing rules for gamblers and gaming must be taken to have superseded the rigid prohibition in the Dharma Śástra of Manu, ch. 9, sl. 220—228.

[307] Manu ch. 8, sl. 274, where the offence is much more leniently dealt with.

[308] The intent of these insulting allusions is obvious.

[309] What we have rendered 'cast' is expressed by two words in the original, *varna* and *játi*. The first is defined by the Commentator—the four casts; the second—the mixed classes or casts.

[310] Manu, ch. 8, sl. 267, 8, 9, 70, 276, 7.

[311] The Commentator instances the buttocks.

lowest fine.

212. If a person be beaten without witnesses, the case shall be tried by marks, probabilities and public report; not however without some suspicion that the marks may have been falsely contrived.

213. For [defiling by] touching with ashes, mud, or dust, a fine is fixed of ten *panas*; for [defiling by] touching with impurities,[312] *scil.* of the heel or of the saliva, double [that fine]:

214. that is, if the parties be on an equality. If [the offence be] against other men's wives, or against superiors, [then the penalty is] double; if against inferiors, the half. Should [the aggressors] be insane or intoxicated or the like, there shall not be punishment.

215. Should a limb of one not a bráhman occasion pain to a bráhman, it shall be cut off. If [a weapon] be raised [against one of inferior cast],[313] the lowest fine [is to be paid]; if the weapon be merely handled, then the fine shall be half.[314]

216. But should a hand or a foot be raised, the fine shall be [respectively] ten and twenty *panas*. People, however, of any [cast, who lift] weapons against their cast-fellows shall pay the middle fine.

217. For pulling a person by the foot, by the hair, by the clothing, or by the hand, the fine is ten *panas*: for inflicting pain by dragging about or by violent handling of the clothes, and for putting the foot upon a person, [the fine is] a hundred *panas*.

218. He who beats with a stick or the like, short of effusion of blood, shall pay a fine of thirty-two *panas*; if blood appear, the fine is double[315]

219. For damaging a hand, a foot, or a tooth, and for cutting the ears or the nose, there is the middle fine: the same for rending open a wound, or for beating a person till he be as one lifeless.

220. For beating [one so that he] cannot stir, or [so that he cannot] eat, or [so that he cannot] speak, for destroying an eye and the like,[316] for breaking a neck, an arm, or a thigh, [there shall be] the middle fine.[317]

221. If several unite in beating one person, the fine shall be double[318] that prescribed; whatever property be taken away in the struggle shall be restored, and, in addition, the double fine [imposed].

222. Whoever causes pain to another [by any such means] shall be made to pay the expense of the cure, as well as the regulated fine for the fray.[319]

223. He who batters, rends, breaks or pulls down a wall, shall be made to pay

[312] such as tears, nails, hair, wax of the ear, &c. (*M.*)
[313] So explained by the Commentator.
[314] Manu, ch. 8, sl. 279, 80.
[315] Manu, ch. 8, sl. 284.
[316] The Commentator instances the tongue.
[317] Manu ch. 8, sl. 284, 286-7.
[318] *i. e.* each wrong doer pays the double fine. (*M.*)
[319] Manu ch. 8, sl. 287.

a fine of five, ten or twenty *panas* besides the value.

224. He who casts into a dwelling house any thing hurtful or destructive of life, shall be made to pay, for the first a fine of sixteen *panas*, for the second the middle fine.

225. For injury to the smaller sort of cattle, or for shedding their blood, for lopping one of their horns or the like[320] or one of their limbs, one shall pay a fine of two and a half *panas* and upwards.

226. For cutting off the male privy member [of such cattle], or slaying [one], the middle fine, as well as the value [of the animal], shall be paid. For the larger cattle in such cases the fine is double.[321]

227. For cutting down branches, or the trunk, or the entire tree,[322] of such as re-produce [after mutilation], [also for similar injuries] to trees which supply food,[323] the fine shall be doubled progressively up from twenty *panas*:[324]

228. should the trees be growing where there are memorial erections, or in places for disposal of the dead, or on boundary lines, or in holy places, or in a temple, a double fine [shall be levied]; so, for any famous tree.[325]

229. For cutting brushwood, grasses, shrubs, climbing plants, ground-spreading creepers, annuals, and herbs, at the places above mentioned, half of the fine is ordained.

230. Forcibly taking away [any thing, though it be] public property, is *sáhasa*;[326] the fine for it is double the value [of the property]. [If the crime be,] on denial, [proved,] then, four times the value.

231. He who instigates the commission of *sáhasa*, shall pay a double fine, and four-fold if he instigate by promise of reward.

232. He who rails at a venerable person,[327] or who disobeys such an one, he who maltreats his brother's wife,[328] he who fails to give that which he has promised, he who forces a dwelling-house with a seal upon it,[329]

233. he who does harm to his neighbour, or to his kindred, and such like[330] — each of these shall be fined fifty *panas*. So is it enjoined.

---

[320] or any other insensitive part, *sákhá*.

[321] Manu ch. 8, sl. 297-8.

[322] root as well as trunk. (*M.*)

[323] *scil.* the mango. (*M.*)

[324] *scil.* 20, 40, 80. (*M.*)

[325] Manu, ch. 8, sl. 285.

[326] This word is commonly used to signify any violent aggression upon person or property, and is defined here by the Commentator to be, the forcibly taking away of property either public or private. Manu, ch. 8, sl. 332.

[327] *e.g.* an *áchárya*. (*M.*) Supra note[‡‡] in fin. The injunction evidently has reference to one whose office or character entitles him to the respect and obedience of those about him, pupils or disciples.

[328] This may be 'his brother or his wife.'

[329] The Commentator does not explain this description.

[330] *scil.* those of the same village or country. (*M.*)

234. He who, [on the impulse] of his own will [merely], goes to a widow,[331] he who, when there is a cry for help, does not haste [to render it], he who reviles without cause, a *chandála*[332] who touches one of higher cast,

235. he who, when making an oblation to the gods or to ancestors, feeds Śúdrás, or *pravrájikas*,[333] he who swears an improper oath, or who does what he has no title to do,[334]

236. he who emasculates a bull or smaller animal, who embezzles common property, who destroys the embryo of a female slave,

237. and, among fathers and sons, sisters and brothers, husbands and wives, teachers and disciples, if either desert the other, [he or she] not being an outcast— [in these several instances,] the fine is a hundred *paṇas*.[335]

238. A washerman who wears another's dress shall be fined three *paṇas*; if he sell, let out, pledge, or, when importuned [give it away],[336] ten *paṇas*.

239. If, when father and son quarrel, one volunteer to be a witness,[337] the fine is three *paṇas*; but, if [on such an occasion] one offer himself as surety,[338] he shall be fined eight-fold.

240. Whoever falsifies scales, or a royal order, or a measure,[339] or a coin,[340] likewise whoever [knowingly] uses them [so falsified], shall be made to pay the highest fine.[341]

241. A tryer of coin who pronounces a false one to be genuine or a genuine one to be false, shall be made to pay the highest fine.

242. One who falsely sets himself up as a physician,[342] shall, [for his malpractice,] if brutes be concerned, pay the first fine—if mankind, the middle fine—but, if royal officers, the highest fine.

243. Whoso imprisons one not deserving of imprisonment,[343] or releases one found worthy of imprisonment or pending his trial,[344] shall pay the highest fine.

[331] *i. e.* when not authorised by the 'Śástras. Supra sl. 127.

[332] An outcast.

[333] The Commentator explains this term here by *digambara*, which is the usual designation of a Buddha mendicant.

[334] as if a Śúdrá teach the Vedas.

[335] Manu inflicts 600 *paṇas*, ch. 8, sl. 389.

[336] Thus the Commentator supplies the ellipsis.

[337] instead of acting as a mediator. (*M.*)

[338] when it is agreed to decide the dispute by a wager, (*M.*)

[339] of quantity, for water, grain, &c.

[340] *náṇáka*, Wilson's *Ariana antiqua* pa. 364. The Commentator defines this word— something stamped with an impression, as a *nishka*—this is a piece of gold of a certain standard or weight.

[341] Manu, ch. 9, sl. 232.

[342] *i. e.* who, though ignorant of the *Ajur Veda* sets up as a practitioner of the medical art. (*M.*) Manu, ch. 9, sl. 284.

[343] The Commentator adds 'without royal authority.'

[344] After having summoned the accused to take his trial. (*M.*) This explanation shows, that the injunction applies to judicial functionaries, although in its terms general.

244. He who, in measurement, or [use of] the scales, defrauds [to the extent] of an eighth, shall be made to pay a fine of two hundred *panas*, and thus proportionably for a more or less quantity.

245. He who adulterates[345] medicine, or oily commodities, or salt, or perfumes, or corn, or sugar, or other saleable articles, shall be fined sixteen *panas*.

246. For making one sort of article to appear to be of another sort, whether it be earthen goods, or skins, or precious stones, or threads, or corn, or wood, or bark of trees, or clothes, a fine [is ordained of] eight-fold the purchase money.

247. For him who changes a covered basket,[346] or who gives in pledge or sells counterfeit drugs in a wrapper,[347] the fines prescribed are,

248. where [the value is] below a *pana* fifty *panas*, where [it amounts to] a *pana* one hundred *panas*, where to two *panas* two hundred *panas*: with increase of value the fine increases.

249. The highest fine is imposed on those who, [although] aware of the rise or fall in prices, combine, to the prejudice of labourers and artists, to create a price [of their own].

250. For traders who combine, by [arbitrarily fixing] an improper price, to impede [the traffic in] any commodity, or to make [an injurious] sale of it,[348] the highest fine is ordained.

251. The price in [transactions of] sale and purchase, daily, is regulated by the monarch;[349] the difference[350] is declared to be the traders' profit.

252. On goods of his own country let a trader clear a profit of five per cent., and ten per cent. on those of another country; provided he make prompt sale of his purchase.

253. [The monarch] is to determine the price, in unison with the wishes of both purchaser and seller; first adding to the cost of the article the expense of bringing it to the market.[351]

254. He who, having received the price of any commodity, fails to deliver it to the buyer, shall be compelled to deliver the article, together with damages [for the detention]; and should the buyer be from foreign parts, then, the foreign profit [shall be added].

255. There may be a re-sale of goods sold, if the original buyer will not receive them. If loss arise from misconduct of the buyer, he shall bear it.

---

[345] literally, adds something inferior to. Manu, ch. 9, sl. 286,7.

[346] *e. g.* substituting a basket of crystals for one of jewels. (*M.*)

[347] as camphor, or musk. (*M.*)

[348] *i. e.* combining to buy up at a low rate some foreign merchandize, or to revend it at a dear rate.

[349] Manu, ch. 8, sl. 398, 401, 2.

[350] *semble* in the daily prices, purchasers and sellers respectively profiting by an increase or diminution of the tariff of prices.

[351] Literally, 'expenses arising out of the commodity,' which the Commentator explains to be, the cost of import, customs-duty, &c.

256. Whatever damage may befal goods by [act of] the monarch, or by accident, shall be the loss of the seller,[352] where he has failed to make delivery on demand.

257. If a person re-sell that which has been sold to another, or sell, as sound, a damaged article; [in either case] the fine shall be double the value [of the article sold].

258. A trader who makes a purchase in ignorance of the rise and fall of prices, must not recede from his bargain; if he do, he shall be fined a sixth [of the price].

259. Traders who carry on business jointly, for profit, shall share the profits and losses, either in proportion to the capital [brought in by each], or according to the contract between them.[353]

260. [A joint trader] who occasions loss [to the partnership] by [engaging in] something which his partner has either prohibited or not sanctioned, or by any negligence, shall make it good: if [on the other hand by his personal exertion] he preserve anything [of the partnership property] from loss, he shall have the tenth of it.[354]

261. The monarch, for fixing the prices, should receive a duty of a twentieth.[355]

If an article of which the sale is prohibited, or one fitting for the monarch[356] [to possess], be sold [without the royal license], it shall be forfeited to the Crown.[357]

262. Whoever declares false weight, or avoids the place where custom is levied, shall be made to pay eight-fold; so he who fraudulently buys or sells.[358]

263. A ferryman levying [toll as though for] land-duties, shall be made to pay a fine of ten *paṇas*.[359]

The same fine is ordained for omission to send invitations to bráhmaṇs of the neighbourhood.[360]

264. On the death of one departed to a foreign country, his male offspring, his maternal kindred, or those more remotely related, shall take the property: in their default, the monarch [succeeds].

265. Let the partners of a man who acts dishonestly exclude him from any share of the profits. Let him who is disabled [to act personally in the partnership

[352] The Commentator adds the condition, 'if he have not repented him of his bargain.'

[353] According to the Commentator this rational liberty of action is not confined to traders; he instances, 'players, dancers, *and the like.*'

[354] *scil.* for himself, separate from his partnership interest.

[355] The same is given by Manu; although the sovereign would appear not to have had, in those earlier days, so responsible or despotic a control of the market, ch. 8, sl. 398, 402.

[356] *i. e.* too good for a mere subject. The Commentator explains, 'jewels, &c.'

[357] ibid. sl. 399.

[358] *scil.* where the property in the goods is disputed. (*M.*) Manu, ch. 8, sl. 400.

[359] Land tolls or duties are a twentieth, and are leviable by the king alone. (*M.*)

[360] on occasion of *sráddahs*, &c. Manu, ch. 8, sl. 392, where a priest for such an offence is fined a silver *másha* (supra B. 1 sl. 363)

business] act by the agency of another. Thus too it is enjoined for [associations of] priests[361] farmers, and craftsmen.

266. Capture of a thief by the officer is warranted by [his possession of] the property stolen, or by traces of him, also by his having been an offender previously, or his being an inmate of a house of ill repute.

267. And others there are who may be arrested on suspicion, *viz.*, such as conceal their caste, name, &c., also those addicted to gambling, to women, and to drinking, and such as have [betrayed themselves by] a parched mouth in speaking, or a stammering voice;

268. those, moreover, who are inquisitive about others' goods and houses, or who put on a disguise, or who expend [lavishly] although they have no [ostensible] income, or who sell things that have been in use.

269. If one arrested on suspicion of theft do not clear himself, he is to be punished as a thief, being first compelled to make good the property stolen.

270. [The monarch] should compel the thief to make restitution of the stolen articles, and subject him to [such of] the different corporeal inflictions [as may be proper]: a bráhmaṇ [who is a thief] he shall brand and banish the realm.

271. When a murder or theft has occurred, and [the criminal] is not traced beyond the village, blame falls on the village governor; if [he be traced] to the public road, blame falls on the governor of the district; if traced out of the district, the officer charged with pursuit of criminals shall be to blame.

272. The village within whose boundary [the crime is perpetrated] shall pay; or [that village shall pay] to which track [of the criminal] leads; so, if the track lead to a place within a *krôsh*[362] skirting five villages [all shall pay]; so of ten villages.

273. House-breakers,[363] they who steal horses or elephants, murderers by open violence—such shall be impaled.

274. He who purloins [apparel, &c.[364]] shall have a hand cut off; cut-purses,[365] shall have the thumb and fore-finger cut off; for a second offence, a hand and a foot shall be cut off.

275. For theft of goods of trifling, of medium, and of the highest value,[366] the penalty to be inflicted is proportioned to the value of what is stolen. In its determination, place, time, age, and ability, are to be considered.[367]

[361] Manu, ch. 8, sl. 207.

[362] a land-measure, *scil.* 4,000 *hâts* or cubits.

[363] The Commentator explains this term by quoting from Manu—"They who break into houses where a sacred fire is kept up, into arsenals, into temples—" ch. 9, sl. 276, 280.

[364] The subject of theft is supplied by the Commentator.

[365] who abstract money from the person by cutting or opening the apparel. Manu, ch. 9, sl. 277; where the third offence entails capital punishment.

[366] *scil.* trifling—such as, earthen vessels, stools, cots, bones, wood, leather, grass, &c.; medium—such as, apparel (other than silk), cattle (other than cows), metal (other than gold), rice, barley; highest—as, gold, jewels, silks, women, men, cows, elephants, horses, also whatever is appropriated to gods, to bráhmaṇs, or to kings. (*M.*)

[367] Manu, ch. 8, sl. 126; supra B. 1, sl. 367.

276. One who knowingly supplies a thief or a murderer with food, shelter, fire, water, counsel, implements, or money, incurs the highest fine.[368]

277. For wounding with weapons, and for causing abortion, the highest fine is ordained; the highest or the lowest for killing a man or a woman.

278. A woman incorrigibly wicked, one who has slain a man, one who has destroyed dams,[369] shall, unless she be in a state of pregnancy, be thrown into [deep] water with a [heavy] stone tied to her.

279. A woman who is a poisoner, or an incendiary, one who has slain her husband, her *guru*, or her child, shall be put to death by bulls, her ears, hands, nose, and lips being cut off.[370]

280. If a man be slain, and it be not known who did the deed, his sons, kindred, wives, also women who are in habits of illicit intercourse, are to be separately and without delay questioned, — as to, whether any quarrel has occurred,

281. whether the deceased was addicted to women, or fond of what is costly, or seeking gain,[371] also with whom he had gone — or, the people in the neighbourhood of the place where the murder occurred shall be examined, by gentle means.

282. Incendiaries of fields, houses, forests, villages, pasture-grounds or granaries, also one who has intercourse with the wife of the king, are to be burned in a straw-fire.

283. A man is to be apprehended for adultery, if [found] with another man's wife in mutual grasping of hair or with recent love-marks, or when both admit [their fault],

284. or [if the man be found] toying with her girdle, with her breasts, her upper garment, her thigh, or her hair, or conversing with her at an unfitting place or hour, or on the same spot with her.[372]

285. The wife, if [so acting] after express prohibition, shall pay one hundred *panas* fine; the man, two hundred *panas*: if both have been expressly prohibited [so demeaning themselves], their punishment shall be the same as for adultery.[373]

286. For adultery with a woman of equal cast, a man incurs the highest fine; with a woman of lower cast, the middle fine; with a woman of higher cast, [the penalty is] death,[374] and the woman is to have her ears, &c.[375] cut off.

287. If one make off with a virgin decked out [for the bridal], he shall pay the highest fine; if she be not so circumstanced, then the lowest fine. Thus it is, if the virgin be of equal cast: if she be of higher cast, [the penalty of] death is ordained.

---

[368] Manu, ch. 9, sl. 278.

[369] thus causing destruction of the crops. Manu, ch. 9, sl. 279.

[370] unless she be pregnant. (*M.*)

[371] These compounds might be literally translated, 'woman-fond' 'thing-fond' 'gain-fond.'

[372] Manu, ch. 8, sl. 356, 7, 8.

[373] ibid. sl. 361.

[374] ibid. sl. 359, 374.

[375] The Commentator explains — her nose, &c.

288. In the case of a virgin consenting and of inferior cast, no offence [is committed]; otherwise, there is a fine.[376] For ravishing her, the man's hand shall be cut off: if the virgin be of the highest cast, [the penalty is] death.

289. Whoso speaks disparagingly of a woman shall forfeit one hundred *panas*; but, two hundred, one who brings a false charge against [a woman]. Whoso has carnal knowledge of a brute animal shall forfeit one hundred *panas*; if of a lowest cast woman[377] or of a cow, the middle fine.

290. If a man[378] have carnal intercourse with female slaves or servants, or even with common women, [such slaves, &c.] being kept [by those to whom they belong] secluded,[379] he shall pay a fine of fifty *panas*.

291. For forcing a female slave,[380] it is written, there shall be a fine of ten *panas*; if many [men so] attack one slave, each one shall pay twenty-four *panas*.

292. A public woman who refuses after taking her hire, shall forfeit twice the amount; so, if the man [decline after contracting, yet] he shall pay.

293. Whoso knows a woman unnaturally, or voids his water upon a man, also one who has carnal knowledge of a female mendicant, shall be fined twenty-four *panas*.

294. [The monarch] shall banish him who goes to a woman of the lowest grade, having branded him with dishonoring emblems: if a Súdrá so act, he shall be [classed among] the lowest. Death shall be to the man of lowest grade who goes to a respectable woman.

295. Whoso fabricates a royal grant,[381] be it for much or little, or sets free one who has kidnapped a woman, shall pay the highest fine.

296. One who brings dishonor to a bráhman by giving as food what is unfit to be eaten, is amenable to the highest fine; if to a kshattriya, the medium fine; if to a vaisyá, the lowest fine; if to Súdrá, half the lowest.

297. If one trade with counterfeit gold, or sell tainted meat; three of his members[382] shall be amputated, and he shall pay the highest fine.

298. Damage caused by four-footed animals shall not be borne by their owner, if he have given warning to clear the way: so, with regard to wood, earth, arrows, stones, a man's arm, or any yoked animals.

299. If death be caused by a vehicle through the breaking of the [animal's] nose-bridle, or through breaking of the yoke, or the like, or from its running backwards, the owner is [to be held] blameless.[383]

300. If the owner of biting or horned animals do not, although able, rescue [a

[376] Manu, ch. 8, sl. 364.
[377] ibid. sl. 373, 385.
[378] *scil.* a stranger.
[379] Manu, ch. 8, sl. 363.
[380] *scil.* one kept for prostitution. (*M.*)
[381] Manu, ch. 9, sl. 232, where this is a capital offence.
[382] The Commentator instances, the nose, ear, and hand. Manu, ch. 9, sl. 292.
[383] Manu, ch. 8, sl. 291, 2.

person attacked], he shall pay the lowest fine: but, if there was a cry for help, then, double that fine.

301. He who calls an adulterer, 'thief,' shall be made to pay a fine of five hundred *panas*: whoever releases such an one, being bribed thereto,[384] shall be made to pay eight-fold the amount [of the bribe].[385]

302. Whoso speaks what is offensive to the monarch, or reproaches the monarch, or divulges the monarch's counsel, shall have his tongue excised and be banished.

303. Whoso makes sale of garments [used to wrap] the dead, or strikes his *guru*, or seats himself on the vehicle or on the seat of the monarch, shall pay the highest fine.

304. Whoso beats out both [a person's] eyes, a bearer of odious tidings to the monarch, also a Śúdrá holding himself out as a bráhman, — [each of these] shall be fined eight hundred *panas*.

305. Such law suits as have been decided unrighteously shall be re-investigated by the monarch: [in case of reversal of the judgment] the judges and the winning party shall be amerced in double the amount of the fine decreed in the suit.

306. Should one defeated on the contest of his suit represent as though he were not defeated, he shall, when he comes [again to urge his suit, besides] being re-defeated, be fined double.

307. Should the monarch have inflicted any fine unjustly, he shall himself, after making invocation to Varuṇa,[386] present thirty times the amount [of the fine] to bráhmaṇs.

---

[384] Literally 'after having taken money.'
[385] Receivers of bribes are denounced in Manu, ch. 9, sl. 258.
[386] Supra, no.[§§].

ENDNOTES

[*]   These are expressed by one word, *kalaha*: but the Commentator notes its comprehensive character, as we have translated it. See the analogous passage in Manu, ch. 8, sl. 6, where an equally ambiguous word *párushya* is similarly explained in the text itself. The term rendered "slander" by Sir Wm. Jones is simply, reviling or verbal abuse.

[†]   Between this and the succeeding sloka another is introduced in the text of the Calcutta edition; *viz.* Possession accompanied by a clear title is proof; possession unaccompanied by a clear title is no proof. — We have omitted this, because the Commentator quotes it as a saying of Nárada, and because it is not found (as vouched by professor Stenzler) in either of the M.S.S. in the Berlin Royal Library.

[‡]   Who these are is described by Yájnavalkya, in the third book, *scil.*

sl. 227. The slayer of a bráhmaṇ, the drinker of what intoxicates, the thief, one who violates his *guru's* bed, are great criminals — also, whoever associates with such persons.

sl. 228. Grossly to revile one's *guru*, speaking reproachfully of the Vedas, to slay a friend, after reading from the Veda to forget it, — these [sins] are like to the murder of a bráhmaṇ.

sl. 229. To eat forbidden food, a crooked insincere mode of dealing, a multitude of lying words, kissing the mouth of a menstruous woman, — these [sins] are like to drinking intoxicating liquor.

sl. 230. To steal horses, jewels, men, women, land, cows, property pledged, — these [sins] are like to the stealing of gold.

sl. 231. To debauch a friend's wife, a maiden, a sister, a woman of the lowest grade, a female relative, a son's wife, — these [sins] are recorded as equivalent to violation of a *guru's* bed.

sl. 232. To debauch a father's sister, or a mother's, the wife of a maternal uncle, a daughter-in-law, a step-mother, the sister or daughter of an *áchárya*,

sl. 233. or his wife, or one's own daughter, — these are equal to violation of a *guru's* bed. The penalty is death, the pudenda [of the criminal] being previously amputated. A like doom is for the woman, if she consented.

See Manu, ch. 9, sl. 235; ch. 11, sl. 54 — 58, sl. 170 — 180.

As to the *guru* and *áchárya*, the following is the 34th sloka of Yájnavalkya's first book: — He is a man's *guru*, who, after going through the ritual, imparts to him the

Veda: he is *áchárya*, who invests with the sacred cord and then imparts the Veda.

[§] See Lassen's *Indische Alterthumskunde*, vol. II, p. 510.

[¶] Pre-eminent, divine sages; probably the great Rishis, the first-created of Brahmá, mentioned in the opening verse of Manu.

In the third book (sl. 186—189) two classes of Munis are described, of whom one, after blessed experience of Heaven, return to Earth, and the other are to continue in the abodes of bliss until the destruction of the universe. These latter are the publishers of the Vedas, Upanishads, Sútras, Puránas, in fine of all records of knowledge through the medium of language.

[**] *dharma* wife is defined by the Commentator, a wife of the same cast with her husband, and wedded to him according to the *bráhma* and other approved forms of marriage; which are described in the first book, sl. 58-61, *viz.* "In the marriage called *bráhma*, [the bride], adorned in a manner suitable to the means [of her family], is bestowed upon the invited bridegroom,—In the *daiva* [marriage, the bride is made over] to the priest whilst offering sacrifice: *ársha* [marriage], is where [the bride's father] receives a pair of kine.—In the *káya* [marriage, the bride] is delivered to the suitor with the injunction, Together practise the rules of duty! In the *asura* [marriage], wealth is received [from the bridegroom]. *Gándharva* is [a union in marriage] by mutual consent [of the parties]: the *rákshasa* [marriage], is by capture [of the woman] in war: the *paiśácha* [marriage, where she is obtained] by deception." Manu ch. 3, sl. 20 *et. seq.*

[††] *scil.* duties prescribed by the Śruti and Smriti, according to their cast and grade. (*M.*)

[‡‡] Who these are is described by Yájnavalkya, in the third book, *scil.*

sl. 227. The slayer of a bráhman, the drinker of what intoxicates, the thief, one who violates his *guru's* bed, are great criminals—also, whoever associates with such persons.

sl. 228. Grossly to revile one's *guru*, speaking reproachfully of the Vedas, to slay a friend, after reading from the Veda to forget it,—these [sins] are like to the murder of a bráhman.

sl. 229. To eat forbidden food, a crooked insincere mode of dealing, a multitude of lying words, kissing the mouth of a menstruous woman,—these [sins] are like to drinking intoxicating liquor.

sl. 230. To steal horses, jewels, men, women, land, cows, property pledged,—these [sins] are like to the stealing of gold.

sl. 231. To debauch a friend's wife, a maiden, a sister, a woman of the lowest grade, a female relative, a son's wife,—these [sins] are recorded as equivalent to violation of a *guru's* bed.

sl. 232. To debauch a father's sister, or a mother's, the wife of a maternal uncle, a daughter-in-law, a step-mother, the sister or daughter of an *áchárya*,

sl. 233. or his wife, or one's own daughter,—these are equal to violation of a *guru's* bed. The penalty is death, the pudenda [of the criminal] being previously amputated. A like doom is for the woman, if she consented.

See Manu, ch. 9, sl. 235; ch. 11, sl. 54—58, sl. 170—180.

As to the *guru* and *áchárya*, the following is the 34th sloka of Yájnavalkya's first book:—He is a man's *guru*, who, after going through the ritual, imparts to him the Veda: he is *áchárya*, who invests with the sacred cord and then imparts the Veda.

[§§]   Manu, ch. 8, sl. 180.

Lector House believes that a society develops through a two-fold approach of continuous learning and adaptation, which is derived from the study of classic literary works spread across the historic timeline of literature records. Therefore, we aim at reviving, repairing and redeveloping all those inaccessible or damaged but historically as well as culturally important literature across subjects so that the future generations may have an opportunity to study and learn from past works to embark upon a journey of creating a better future.

This book is a result of an effort made by Lector House towards making a contribution to the preservation and repair of original ancient works which might hold historical significance to the approach of continuous learning across subjects.

HAPPY READING & LEARNING!

LECTOR HOUSE LLP
E-MAIL: lectorpublishing@gmail.com

www.ingramcontent.com/pod-product-compliance
Lightning Source LLC
LaVergne TN
LVHW091148180726
843490LV00004B/1373